Levinas and the Wisdom of Love

Levinas and the Wisdom of Love

The Question of Invisibility

Corey Beals

BAYLOR UNIVERSITY PRESS

Cover Design by Pam Poll

Library of Congress Cataloging-in-Publication Data

Beals, Corey.
  Lévinas and the wisdom of love : the question of invisibility / Corey Beals.
    p. cm.
  Includes bibliographical references (p.   ) and index.
  ISBN 978-1-932792-59-1 (cloth : alk. paper)
  1. Lévinas, Emmanuel. 2. Love. I. Title.

  B2430.L484B43 2007
  194--dc22
                                    2007028560

To

Samuel (13 years old) who showed me how
to listen to God's voice

and to

Emmanuel (10 years old) who showed me how
to recognize God's presence

Contents

Acknowledgments

I began writing this book in the Bronx, New York, wrote much of it in New Haven, Connecticut, and finished writing it in Newberg, Oregon. I have many to thank in each place. In the Bronx, I am very grateful to John Drummond, Dana Miller, Chris Cullen, and especially to John Davenport for his thorough reading and comments, and most of all to Merold Westphal for his always prompt and highly helpful comments on each of the chapters. I also thank Maria Terzulli for easing the logistical difficulties of cross-coastal communication.

In New Haven, I am filled with deep appreciation to our community housemates, Mark Totten and Kristin Rinehart-Totten, for listening to me talk at the dinner table about that day's writing challenges, and for helping in the journey out of autonomy. I am also thankful to Todd Buras, Andrew Dole, Todd O'Hara, and the rest of the philosophy of religion weekly lunch group in New Haven for engaging in discussions about Levinas.

In Newberg, I am quite grateful to our community at George Fox University. I thank Richard Engnell, Mark McLeod, Phil Smith, Paul Anderson, and Howard Macy who have read or heard parts of my work and provided encouragement in the writing process. My collegial relationships with these and others at George Fox are a source of joy and inspiration. I thank, too, my philosophy students in the Levinas seminar for engaging my work. To see them enter into these ideas with more than their minds and see them digest this philosophy and live differently has provided me more joy than they will know.

I am grateful to George Fox University for research grants during two summers to continue work on this book and also to Reedwood Friends for sponsoring my research through their Scholar-in-Residence program. Engaging discourse on Levinas in these settings helped me encounter Levinas and others without the technical nomenclature and helped Levinas sink in more deeply than ever before. I thank two Quaker retreat centers, Twin Rocks on the coast and especially Tilikum just outside of Newberg, for providing a place that allows sustained, quiet reflection.

I am thankful for Gregg Koskela as well as the men's group with whom I meet regularly for providing a place to practice the journey from invisibility to visibility. It is impossible for me to adequately acknowledge my parents for they have shown me what it means to be for others. Their lives are testimony to how one can live life in asymmetrical love for the other. Though I can never fully return gratitude, I thank them, nonetheless.

Most of all, I express my greatest gratitude and deepest love to my wife, Jillian, with whom I have been in each place. Moving across the country, leaving family behind and making innumerable sacrifices on many scales, she has inspired me, encouraged me, loved me, and taught me—she has been to me the discreet Other.

It seems like completing this book should be a moment of autonomous accomplishment, but instead it is a moment of realizing that without so many others I do not do what I do and I am not who I am. It is, therefore, a time of recognizing my heteronomy—and the thought of it is terrible, but the living of it is terribly good.

List of Abbreviations

English Translations

AT	Alterity and Transcendence
BPW	Basic Philosophical Writings
BV	Beyond the Verse: Talmudic Readings and Lectures
CP	Collected Papers
DEH	Discovering Existence with Husserl
DF	Difficult Freedom: Essays on Judaism
DL	Dialogues with Contemporary Continental Thinkers: Levinas
DR	"Diachrony and Representation" in EN
DTO	"Dialogue on Thinking-of-the-Other" in EN
EFP	"Ethics as First Philosophy" in LR
EI	Ethics and Infinity: Conversations with Philippe Nemo
EN	Entre Nous: On Thinking-of-the-Other
FOO	"From the One to the Other" in EN
FPC	French Philosophers in Conversation
GCM	Of God Who Comes to Mind
GDT	God, Death, and Time
GP	"God and Philosophy" in BPW
GT	"The Glory of Testimony" in EI
IT	"The I and the Totality" in EN
LR	The Levinas Reader

MS   "Meaning and Sense" in BPW
NC   "Nonintentional Consciousness" in EN
NTR   Nine Talmudic Readings
OB   Otherwise than Being
OS   Outside the Subject
OT   "From One to the Other" in EN
OUJ   "The Other, Utopia, and Justice" in EN
PAR   "The Prohibition against Representation" in AT
PM   "The Paradox of Morality" in PL
PN   Proper Names
PL   The Provocation of Levinas
PJL   "Philosophy, Justice, and Love" in EN
PO   "The Proximity of the Other" in AT
PP   "Peace and Proximity" in AT
PT   "Philosophy and Transcendence" in AT
TDT   "Truth of Disclosure and Truth of Testimony" in BPW
TI   Totality and Infinity
TIPG   Totality and Infinity: "Preface to the German Edition" in EN
TIHP   The Theory of Intuition in Husserl's Phenomenology
TO   Time and the Other
TN   In the Time of Nations
UN   "Uniqueness" in EN
US   "Useless Suffering" in EN
VF   "Violence of the Face" in AT

French Texts

AE   Autrement Qu'être Ou Au-Delà De L'essence
AeT   Altérité et transcendence
AV   L'au-delà du verset: Lectures et discours talmudiques
DE   De l'evasion
DEE   De l'existence à l'existant
DL   Difficile liberté
DMT   Dieu, la mort et le temps
DVI   De Dieu qui vient à l'idée
EDH   En découvrant l'existence avec Husserl et Heidegger
EeI   Ethique et infini
ENP   Entre Nous: Essais sur le penser-à-l'autre
HN   A l'heure des nations
HS   Hors sujet

NP	Noms propres
PeP	"Paix et proximité"
TeI	Totalité Et Infini, Essai Sur L'extériorité
TIH	Théorie de l'intuition dans la phenomenology de Husserl

Introduction

It is widely acknowledged that Emmanuel Levinas's central claim was the priority of the ethical relation over ontology. There is wide disagreement, however, as to what this means and as to whether it is possible, and if so, how it is possible. Some take Levinas to be saying that we must abandon philosophical wisdom, and others say that the type of wisdom that Levinas advocates is impossible. I will structure a discourse on these questions (and the host of questions that arise along the way) around a central saying of Levinas: "la philosophie: sagesse de l'amour au service de l'amour"[1] (AE, 207) [philosophy is the wisdom of love at the service of love (OB, 162)].

In chapter 1, I will examine Levinas's treatment of *invisibility* as a way to clarify the central questions that arise in relation to Levinas's wisdom of love. The discussion of invisibility will give an overview of the varying interpretations of Levinas's wisdom of love along with the various problems and objections facing each view. Looking at invisibility will set the scene for the subsequent analysis of Levinas's "wisdom of love at the service of love."

Then, in chapter 2, I will identify a vast number of terms related to the concepts in this phrase. I will address the terminology used by Levinas across his corpus and ask why he used the terms he did, and how that usage relates to his understanding of philosophy. After identifying this large set of terms related to wisdom and love, I will then ask how some of those terms are similar and how Levinas uses this nomenclature in a unique way. By providing groupings of terms with provisional definitions, I not only seek to bring some clarity to his difficult writing style, but I lay the groundwork for interpretive arguments made in later chapters.

1

In the next three chapters, I will focus on Levinas's understanding of each of the key terms in that saying (chapter 3 is on 'l'amour,' chapter 4 is on 'service,' and chapter 5 is on 'sagesse') as a way of organizing my analysis of Levinas's views on love, wisdom, and the priority relation of wisdom serving love. In chapter 3, I will focus on Levinas's understanding of 'love,' with special attention given to the two types of love: *desire* (as a-satiable desire, or neighbor love) and *need* (as satiable desire, or self love). I will ask whether desire and need as Levinas uses the terms are irreducibly distinct, and if so, whether Levinas thought such a nonreductionist desire was possible. I will then ask if Levinas thought desire and need were compatible, and if so, in what way? I will press the question of how compatibilism of desire and need might be consistent with Levinas's insistence upon the asymmetrical nature of desire, and argue for a nonreductionistic, asymmetrical compatibilism that is not just an impossible ideal, but a possible actuality.

In chapter 4, I will focus on Levinas's understanding of the priority relationship Levinas uses when he says that philosophy is the wisdom of love at the *service* of love. I will examine the possibilities of chronological priority, logical priority, and finally, hierarchical priority. I will argue that he meant the latter but that the change in hierarchical priority he called for was not a mere reversal of hierarchy. I will introduce and defend a type of hierarchical priority that I call a 'pacific inversion of priority.' Such a view of priority, however, requires the important but often ignored distinction between authority and power.

In chapter 5, I will turn to Levinas's understanding of wisdom. I will ask whether Levinas thought wisdom is possible and explain the conditions that Levinas saw as making wisdom not only possible but necessary. If wisdom is necessary, though, how is the wisdom of love Levinas highlights any different than other types of wisdom? The most important answer to that question is a question—Gyges' question that asks, "Is it better to suffer or to inflict injustice?" Wisdom of love, I argue, yields a different answer to that question than wisdoms that trace their origin differently. Breaking Gyges' secret and losing one's invisibility is the heart of Levinas's project, and rightly so, I argue. I turn to actual examples of wisdom answering Gyges' question differently to demonstrate that not only is such a wisdom of love possible, but it is ordinary.

Finally, in chapter 6, I will ask how the scale of wisdom is conducive to or undermining of a wisdom of love. Does the size of group or community in which we gather and associate have some important bearing on whether Gyges' secret is protected or broken? I ask whether smaller scales of wisdom and justice might not be more conducive to wisdom of love than larger scales.

Chapter 1

Levinas and Invisibility

You have trusted in your wickedness and have said, "*No one sees me.*"
Your wisdom and knowledge mislead you when you say to yourself,
"I am, and there *is none besides me.*"

Isaiah 47:10

§1 Histories of Invisibility

Levinas draws from two sources—one traced to Jerusalem and the other to Athens—which both have histories whose opening pages involve invisibility. The Greek historian Herodotus, often referred to as the "father of history,"[1] opens his famous work, *Histories*,[2] with an account of Gyges, who was a servant to Phrygian king Kandaules in the seventh century B.C.E. Gyges is enticed by king Kandaules to hide behind a screen to observe his wife undressing in order to confirm to him that she is the most beautiful of women. Gyges hesitates but eventually does as his king requests only to be noticed by the queen who, angered, later calls him in and tells him that she will either have him killed or require that he kill the king in revenge for this indecency. Gyges, not surprisingly, takes the option to kill the king and once again hides behind the screen in the royal chamber—this time using his invisibility to strike king Kandaules dead while in bed. The result of these acts of invisibility is that he marries the queen and becomes the king, beginning a new royal dynasty that lasts for many generations.

Like this first story in the Greek history, the first human story in the Hebrew history also involves invisibility. After eating the forbidden fruit, Adam and Eve both cover themselves in an attempt to hide their nakedness, and they also hide in the garden, attempting to become invisible to God. It is interesting that in both accounts invisibility is attempted, though not achieved. In the Greek history, however, Gyges' hiding is ultimately rewarded, while in the Judaic history, Adam and Eve's hiding is followed by severe consequences, and the very place in which they sought invisibility was permanently hidden from them. Gyges gets to enter into and possess that which he observes from behind the screen of invisibility. But that which Adam and Eve see with new understanding is taken from them. The Hellenistic story is one of using invisibility to possess what one did not possess, while the Hebrew story is one of invisibility leading to a dispossession.

So how does Levinas, who draws from both of these traditions, treat invisibility? First, I should note that Levinas refers to visibility primarily as a visibility of conceptual understanding, which also can refer to a linguistic expression of that understanding. Colloquially, this view of visibility is commonly experienced when someone says in a moment of comprehension, "Oh, now I see what you mean." Visibility, as used here, is equated with cognition.

As such, which tradition does Levinas draw from in his treatment of invisibility? Does he endorse the tradition that opposes invisibility, or the tradition that rewards it? It is not surprising that the Jewish Levinas most centrally is opposed to his own invisibility and inveighs against its harms to himself and to the Other. But he goes further than just opposing his own invisibility while keeping the Other visible. He speaks of the need to preserve the invisibility of the Other. To see the Other is to think of the Other in terms of a category or a theme, and Levinas shows us that the Other is irreducible to any category of thought—the Other always exceeds any concept I might try to use to 'capture' or understand her.

In *Totality and Infinity*, he even calls the Other 'invisible' and says that the "Invisible is the very elevation of height and its nobility" (35). But we quickly see that what he means by invisibility is not a simple absence of the Other. Instead, the invisibility of the other points to the impossibility of a complete reduction of the Other to a concept. As Levinas is using the term, "invisibility does not denote an absence of relation; it implies relations with what is not given" (TI, 34).

§2 Asymmetrical Vision

But the question that deserves close attention is how my visibility relates to the invisibility of the Other with whom I am in relation. Levinas's analysis of the ethical relation with the Other is radically asymmetrical in that he describes the Other as invisible to my comprehension, while not claiming invisibility for himself. But if to conceptualize or speak conceptually of the Other is to do harm to the Other, where does that leave philosophy? Where does that leave wisdom? If wisdom involves reducing the irreducible Other to cognitive categories, then should philosophy be put to rest? The answers to this question within Levinas scholarship are manifold, and the variety of interpretations urges further consideration.

The fact that Levinas speaks of a way of doing philosophy that is a "wisdom of love at the service of love" (OB, 162) clearly shows that Levinas thought it is allowable for philosophy to continue in some form. The question is what form that philosophy might take. Is Levinas's wisdom of love a wisdom that is done while seeking an impossible ideal of keeping the Other invisible? Is Levinas's point that wisdom is always evil but that it is a necessary evil?

Such a view is argued by Derrida and Others who see the "plea to have the Other remain invisible" as a hyperbolic plea to minimize the necessary damage that is done by wisdom. I consider these sets of interpretations more thoroughly in chapter 3. But ultimately I find that such an interpretation ignores a key variable in the ethical relation—the entrance of the 'third.' It is important to remember that philosophy or wisdom is only born out of a consideration for the third. If there was only one other person in the world, I would be infinitely responsible for that person and any attempt at using philosophy would be an attempt to limit that responsibility and would be a form of legitimizing negligence to the Other. But as soon as a third person arrives on the scene, I now find that I need to understand (or make visible) the Other and the third so that I can decide whom to serve first. While the Other remains invisible when I am alone with the Other and there is no third, the arrival of the third requires that I conceptually 'see' both the Other and the third. And this is not a form of violent excuse-making—rather it is born out of the peaceful need to make wise judgments about serving others. This is what I argue Levinas means by a 'wisdom of love' serving love. It is not wisdom for the sake of being wise, or for the sake of rationalizing negligent or active violence to others. This is the way, contra Derrida, that wisdom can be an actual way of engaging the Other without doing violence.

While I will discuss this in detail in chapter 3, I point to this group of interpretations to show, by contrast, what Levinas is *not* suggesting. He is not suggesting that thought, wisdom, and speech are inherently violent. Invisibility is not required once the third arrives, so there is a way of 'seeing' the Other that is a pacific wisdom of love.

§3 Wisdoms of Love

There is a small but growing number of Levinas scholars who are acknowledging this possibility of a wisdom of love that is neither an impossible, hyperbolic ideal nor a necessary evil. For example, both Alain Finkielkraut and Roger Burggraeve have written books that even use the phrase 'wisdom of love' in the title.[3] They both are right, in my view, to depart from the frequently heard Derridean interpretation and insist that there is a way in which the Other can be visible without violence. A danger that arises, however, when suggesting that Levinas allows for a possible and actual wisdom of love is to do so at the cost of my asymmetrical responsibility for the Other. Is the only way to achieve a wisdom of love to do so on a basis of mutuality? Must I leave behind the asymmetrical nature of my responsibility for the Other once the third arrives on the scene? The third is the birth of wisdom and thought, but is the third the birth of mutuality? Levinas does not, in my view, hold that the introduction of the third entails mutuality. An important form of asymmetry remains even after the third arrives along with the Other. While Finkielkraut's and Burggraeve's views of the wisdom of love make an important advance over the Derridean interpretations, it becomes tempting to achieve this wisdom at the expense of asymmetry. Finkielkraut denies that Levinas is a philosopher of altruism, and says that he only appears that way.[4] I will argue in chapter 3 that Levinas is a philosopher of altruism, even if it is a nuanced form of altruism. Similarly, Burggraeve argues that when the third arrives, and we enter into this wisdom of love, the asymmetry disappears and "symmetry enters." I can now say that I am "an Other like the Others" and we "stand equally before one another."[5] I will argue in chapter 3 and show examples in chapter 5 that while Levinas thinks that the entrance of the third *changes* the asymmetry, it does not *eliminate* it. It is true that the wisdom of love allows for the Other to be 'seen,' but my visibility to the Other and the Other's invisibility to me are not mirror images. There is a significant difference in these types of visibility—it is not as simple as reciprocal sight. In later chapters, my major task will be to show how it is possible to have a wisdom of love that maintains an asymmetrical visibility.

When Finkielkraut and Burggraeve speak of a wisdom of love, it is clear that 'wisdom of love' includes a way of seeing the Other ethically and politically. There are differing opinions, however, on the question of whether Levinas is prohibiting or prescribing a particular ethical/political theory. While the Derridean interpretation of Levinas suggests that no political theory can be just, except the rupturing of unjust theories, Finkielkraut and Burggraeve are right, in my view, to challenge a prohibition of politics. This can be seen across the entire Levinas corpus, as I discuss in chapter 5, but this is especially evident in the later writings. However, to say that Levinas is not prohibiting politics does not entail the view that he is prescribing any one particular political theory.

I argue, however, that Levinas's project is not primarily the promotion of a first-order ethical or political theory. Once one sees that Levinas's ethical metaphysics allows for political theory, it is tempting to guess at what that theory is. This temptation is fed by the fact that Levinas held particular political views. But still, in assessing Levinas's philosophical project, I cannot see that he is offering a first-order political theory. It is more accurate to say that Levinas is providing a "prolegomena to any future politics." His ethical metaphysics is a grounding for a wisdom of love—for ethical or political theories and practices. But his task is not primarily one of building on that foundation.

In the discussions of wisdom of love by both Finkielkraut and Burggraeve, significant attention is given to describing a first-order Levinasian politics. Insofar as these projects are describing how Levinas's views *might* be applied, I do not see that as a problem. But there are times when these authors seem to be suggesting that Levinas was primarily about promoting a particular brand of political philosophy. And if this is so, then it is missing the point that there might be several political theories that fittingly find their grounding in a Levinasian ethical metaphysics. The significant contrast is not so much on the level of first-order politics as it is on the level of grounding, such that the key contrast is not between a universal democracy and some other political theory so much as it is a contrast between a theory whose origin is traced to a Levinasian account of the birth of politics and a theory whose origin is traced to, say, a Hobbesian account of the birth of politics.

Finkielkraut, for example, seeks to provide a return to a political approach he calls a 'critical cultural universalism,' which avoids celebrating difference at the expense of universalism, but also rejects the easy universalism of the American neoconservatives.[6] Burggraeve also offers a concrete political picture, focusing on worldwide human rights. He writes that the "final aim of universal responsibility is a worldwide community in which all people are equal" and envisions that this "human society" has a "global dimension."[7] Levinas clearly had political views himself, and I do not find the political visions of either Burrgraeve or Finkielkraut to be fundamentally in conflict with a Levinasian ethical metaphysics; they are, in fact, excellent explorations into what political fruit might be born from such roots. It is important to note, nonetheless, that these political views are not entailed in Levinas's origin of politics.

Furthermore, the fact that both these political visions are political visions emphasizing equality (including my demanding equality for myself) is a reflection of how they understand the loss of asymmetry in the relation with the Other once the third arrives. While my treatment of the wisdom of love shares the view that Levinas does not absolutely prohibit politics, I depart from them on the nature of the relation with the Other once the third arrives. While seeing the Other and being seen by the Other is allowed, I am suggesting a different relation between the seer and the seen. At least for me, I must maintain my asymmetrical relation with the Other. The implications I draw politically, while not necessarily different from theirs, are not the focus of this present work. I do point to some ways in which this ethical relation makes a radical difference even after the third has arrived. But nonetheless, I am focusing my attention on the origins of visibility, since how my vision begins affects how I see.

§4 Who Cares?

For whom might this question of invisibility be a concern? The fascination with the means and consequences of invisibility appears early in both Hellenistic and Jewish histories, but the fascination does not disappear. Levinas not only addresses invisibility in terms philosophical and religious,[8] but in terms that are simply human. He sums his philosophy saying, "this is my entire philosophy—there is something more important than my life, and that is the life of the other."[9] The fact that this question is a pervasively human question is witnessed by multiple and various cultural expressions.

For example, H. G. Wells in *The Invisible Man* presents the unforeseen consequences of one man who attains the invisibility he so longed for—once invisible, he can no longer become visible, and even though his body is invisible, his impact on the world is always noticed, and ultimately, it creates more of a burden than a freedom for him.

In a less obvious form of invisibility, Alfred Hitchcock in *Rear Window* depicts the strong desire to watch others while remaining unseen and hidden. And even though the 'unseen seer' watches from a distance through binoculars, it quickly becomes apparent that it is not possible to remain detached from what we observe, after all.

George Orwell in *1984* imagines the evils that could be done to a society by a government with the capacity to watch constantly—through surveillance—every move of every citizen while remaining unwatched. Big Brother is the unwatched watcher who is invisible, even though to "him," everyone is visible. Here, the link between invisibility and the violence it enables is strong and memorable.

And of course, J. R. R. Tolkien in *The Lord of the Rings* describes an entire world that rises or falls based on the fate of a ring that renders its bearer invisible. The ring allows the one who wears it the ability to be invisible and this brings obvious powers with it, even though serious consequences result from wearing it. All depends, in the end, on destroying this ring and the ability it gives its bearer to be invisible to the Other.

This invisibility, though philosophical and conceptual, is not disconnected from more mundane manifestations of the desire to disappear. Levinas is calling into question a culture that has for several centuries sought knowledge according to the ideal of the detached observer—the unwatched watcher. Is it surprising that this model of knowing has led to contemporary ways of interacting with each other that include tinted windows, online chat rooms, voyeuristic reality shows, and ubiquitous surveillance cameras?

Much could be said about these and other daily treatments of invisibility, both philosophical, religious, and literary.[10] My focus on Levinas's treatment of the invisible, however, is to use it as a key to comparing the competing interpretations of Levinas. I hope this can serve to further the discussion in Levinas scholarship, but I also hope it can serve as an accessible introduction to Levinas for students and others.

Chapter 2

Levinasian Terminology
La philosophie: sagesse de l'amour au service de l'amour

In this second chapter, I will attempt to bring together a wide array of terminology used by Levinas across a broad selection of his corpus. I will group them according to the ways in which Levinas has used the terms similarly, and I will also be providing approximate or provisional definitions to help bring some clarity to terminology and a writing style that can be quite baffling at times. Why is it worthwhile to include such a chapter in this work? The texts of Levinas are "notoriously difficult," and part of that difficulty results from the fact that new "terms are constantly being adopted and familiar words seem to be used in unfamiliar ways."[1] That might be reason enough, but not all books on Levinas need to include such a chapter, so why have I chosen to do so? I have chosen to include this chapter because clarifying the terminology is crucial to the primary goals of this project mentioned in the introduction. I will briefly explain how.

There are at least three responses to the claim that Levinasian texts are "notoriously difficult." One reader might say that indeed, they are difficult, and delightfully or even necessarily so. A second reader might respond, saying that yes, they are difficult, and painfully so. A third reader might say that, in fact, they are not that difficult at all. I offer a reason for each of these three readers as to why a chapter on terminology is important for this book.

The reader who delights in the difficulty might argue that the way Levinas writes is a necessary part of his philosophy. For example, Colin Davis claims that "the difficulty of Levinas's writing is essential to the paradoxical attempt to think outside the philosophical history to which he knows he also

11

belongs."[2] Such a reader may object that attempting to clarify his terminology is dangerously close to practicing the very type of philosophy Levinas critiques. To such a reader, I say that I do not deny the fact that the form of what is said comprises part of the content. In fact, in chapter 5 I will argue that only some forms of speech are truly consistent with Levinas's wisdom of love, and that these include testimony, teaching, and prophecy.

Even if one acknowledges that the difficult terminology comprises a necessary part of Levinas's philosophy when communicating to some readers, that is not to say that such terminology is necessary for all readers. Insofar as Levinas was engaging those who are offended by perspicuous philosophy, it was perhaps necessary for him to write as he did. There are those who think that "ethics seems trivial, secondary, even a matter for the not-so-smart scholars."[3] Such philosophers who prefer the aesthetic over the ethical are not likely to respect anything that appears too facile. Perhaps it was with such an aesthetically inclined audience in mind that Levinas wrote with such fluidity of language and ambiguity of terminology; if he were to have written plainly, his words might not be welcomed by such readers.[4]

To this reader who appreciates ambiguity, I will say that I am not attempting to reduce all that Levinas said into a few terms and definitions. I do not pretend in the following treatment of terms to capture the richness encountered in the pages of Levinas. To this aesthetic reader, I can best explain the task of this chapter by appealing to aesthetics and diversity. Although the aesthete may not care to see Levinas presented as philosophically perspicuous, there are some for whom clarity and coherence are appreciated not only for practical reasons, but for aesthetic reasons. Thus, to the aesthete, I ask that you tolerate the following attempt at clarity for the pleasure of seeing someone else find pleasure.

To the reader who appreciates clarity and for that reason dismisses or avoids Levinas due to the appearance of obfuscation, I take on the task of this chapter in order to show that there is a coherent philosophy in Levinas that can be communicated clearly. If you are a reader who holds logical coherence dear, and have rejected Levinas due to apparent contradiction, I ask you to reconsider. I will argue that beneath the difficult terminology is coherence, and I will argue this by showing that the terminology is not as prohibitive as it seems. If you are inclined to dismiss an author whose texts "seem calculated . . . to disorientate the reader, to delay rather than to facilitate understanding,"[5] then consider the explanation above as to why Levinas wrote as he did. If his primary audience was one for whom simplicity of diction was cause for dismissal, could it be that he was not seeking obfuscation as his ultimate goal, but that by approaching his reader indirectly, he hoped to treat her with respect? What an analytical philosopher might take as refreshing clarity, an aesthete might take as condescending or banal. Thus, rather than trying to hide weak arguments behind ambiguous language, does it not seem plausible that Levinas knew his profound prophecy would be rejected by some if presented straightforwardly? Thus, his apparent obfuscation may best be explained as having the ultimate goal of clarity, which could only be achieved through the means of prima facie obscurity. Thus, I appeal to you, the lover of clarity, to grant the possibility that Levinas could be shown to hold a coherent view and that the profound testimony he gives is one that can be stated clearly.

Finally, there are those who do not see Levinas as difficult, but suggest that he is simply saying the same thing over and over. For example, after reading *Totality and Infinity*, Jacques Derrida said that it "proceeds with the infinite insistence of waves on a beach,"[6] by which he means that Levinas is just incessantly repeating the same point. Richard Bernstein takes up this metaphor and agrees that Levinas is persistently repetitious.[7] Simon Critchley uses a different metaphor to make the same point—he says that Levinas is like the philosophical hedgehog (who has one big thing to say) rather than the philosophical fox (who says many small things).[8] To such a reader as this, it would seem that the task of terminological clarity attempted in this chapter is superfluous, since he may already be convinced that Levinas is not saying many different things with this terminology, but one big thing. But the following may still be of interest to such a reader, because even though we may agree that Levinas is saying one big thing, there is not agreement as to what that one big thing is. All might agree that the one big thing Levinas says is that ethics is prior to ontology, but there is disagreement as to what that means. Seeing how the various terminologies connect within and between many texts is crucial to the interpretation I will defend, and thus this part of the project may be relevant even to the reader who sees Levinas as repeatedly saying one big thing in many different ways.

In any case, most will agree that the reader of Levinas encounters "terms that are either invented or reallocated meaning by Levinas."[9] It is my goal to help make some sense of this "proliferation of terms" without suppressing the importance of the nuance that such a multiplicity affords. I do not seek to reduce Levinas's philosophy to a simple conclusion, but to show how a clear grouping of his terms brings to light the clarity of his central point. I will organize these terms around a key Levinasian statement and will then use the terms therein to introduce the various families of terms. The important phrase to which I refer is: "Philosophy is the wisdom of love at the service of love" (OB, 162)[10] and this single statement will serve as an organizing principle throughout this entire work. First, I will look at the terms grouped around wisdom and then I will turn to the group of terms clustered about love.

§1. 'Wisdom' [Sagesse] Terminology

'Wisdom' Terminology: in General

When Levinas says that philosophy is the wisdom of love at the service of love, what does he mean by the term 'wisdom'? I should begin by noting that the term wisdom takes neither a place of unqualified honor nor of unqualified critique in his work. Some of the many terms associated with the general term wisdom include 'the third,' 'justice,' 'judgment,' 'comparison,' 'measure,' 'weighing,' 'Said,' 'thematization,' 'thought,' 'knowledge,' 'intelligence,' 'reason,' 'consciousness,' 'ontology,' 'being,' 'comprehension,' 'conceptualization,' 'cognition,' 'politics,' 'the State,' 'institutions,' 'legislation,' 'law,' and 'philosophy.' It is important to note that these terms are closely linked in a way that will aid recognition of the integrity of Levinas's work. In this section, I will present texts that show that these terms are indeed linked, and I will also provide texts that suggest definitions[11] of the various terms. I will present these various wisdom terms in seven groupings; and each of these groups is related to the Other.

Given that these terms are closely linked, it would be easy to conclude that when he speaks critically of wisdom, philosophy, or politics, Levinas is critical of all forms of wisdom, philosophy, and politics. But in fact, the general term 'wisdom' and associated terms are presented in two forms—one of which he is critical; the Other of which he is not. One way Levinas characterizes the contrast between these two wisdoms is by juxtaposing a 'love of wisdom' and a 'wisdom of love.' Levinas writes, "'the love-of-wisdom,' or the love that is the philosophy of Greeks, was the certainty of fields of knowledge directed toward the object, or the even greater certainty of reflection on these fields of knowledge; or whether knowledge beloved of and expected from philosophers was not, beyond the wisdom of such knowledge, the wisdom of love, or wisdom in the guise of love. Philosophy as the love of love" (TIPG, 200). Most of the terms that follow are used in some places to refer both to a love of wisdom and yet in other contexts refer to a wisdom of love. Much of chapter 5 will be devoted to addressing the distinction between 'love of wisdom' and 'wisdom of love' as well as providing examples of the latter. The main goal here is to show that Levinas links these various terms in some way to the more general term 'wisdom' which includes 'wisdom of love' as well as 'love of wisdom.'

Third (le Tiers)

We repeatedly see the term 'wisdom' connected with 'the third' or 'concern for the third' ('le souci du tiers') as when Levinas writes that the relation to "a third party [tiers] . . . is likewise the birth of philosophy as the wisdom of love" (GDT, 183).[12] This relation to the third is defined in relation to the Other[13] for whom I have infinite responsibility. This responsibility for the Other "is troubled and becomes a problem when a third party enters. The third party is other than the neighbor, but also another neighbor, and also a neighbor of the other" (OB, 157). If there is only I and the Other, then I am infinitely responsible for the Other, but when the third appears on the scene, there is the need for comparing the third and the Other in order to judge how to divide my responsibility between them. From the introduction of the third arises a whole host of terms. "The relationship with the third [requires] *weighing, thought, objectification*" (OB, 158; my emphasis). And "the third party calls for . . . a search for *justice*, society and the *State, comparison* and *possession, thought* and *science*, commerce and *philosophy*, and outside of anarchy, the search for a *principle*" (OB, 161; my emphasis). Furthermore, the introduction "of the third party . . . is the moment of justice [which makes] appeal to a *Reason* capable of comparing incomparables, a *wisdom* of love" (UN, 195; my emphasis).[14]

Justice (la Justice)

As seen in the above passages, the first term often used in relation to the introduction of the 'third' is 'justice' (*la justice*).[15] "The *third* party is [the] . . . [b]irth of the question. The first question . . . is the question of justice" (PP, 143; my emphasis). And to the idea that I am infinitely responsible for the Other—"without contradicting it—I immediately add the concern for the *third*, and hence, *justice*" (PJL, 105; my emphasis). Levinas comes close to a definition of justice when he says that justice is "a terrain common to me and the others where I am counted among them . . . with all the duties and rights measured and measurable" (OB, 160). So we see that a key feature of justice is comparison.

Comparison (la Comparaison)

Comparison, along with some other similar terms—measure and weighing—are found frequently in association with 'justice.' What does Levinas mean by comparison, measure, and weighing? First, we can look at what he calls measurement—described as a 'measure' (*mesure*) of obligation. "Philosophy circumscribes the life of the approach and it measures obligation before the third party with justice and knowledge, with wisdom" (OB, 168). The potential point of conflict for Levinas is that the infinite and immeasurable Other must be measured. This is also described in terms of 'comparison' (*la comparaison*)—a comparing of the Other and the third.

Despite the apparent contradiction of comparing the incomparable,[16] comparison is only unjust when the third is not present. However, since there is "always a third party in the world . . . it is important to me to know which of the two takes precedence" and this requires that "human beings, who are incomparable, be compared" (PJL, 104). The Other is 'incomparable' in that he can never be reduced and fully conceptualized, yet when there is more than one Other, they must be compared to know how to divide my responsibility between them. This comparing involves placing two unique Others in a single conceptual genre. "[W]ith the appearance of the third . . . I am led to compare the faces, to compare the two people. Which is a terrible task . . . To compare them is to place them in the same genre" (PM, 174). This comparison, however, is not a destruction of the uniqueness of the two being compared, but it is a placing of "two unique beings" into one genre (PM, 174) without destroying their uniqueness.

Along with measuring and comparing, justice requires a 'weighing' (*pesée*) of the Other and the third. "The relationship with the third party is an incessant correction of the asymmetry of proximity in which the face is looked at. There is *weighing*" (OB, 158; my emphasis). When the third arrives, "I must judge, where before I was to assume responsibilities. . . . At a certain moment, there is a necessity for a 'weighing,' a comparison, a pondering" (PJL, 104). Here we see the tension between 'assuming responsibilities' and 'weighing responsibilities,' and even though the fear is that the latter will (and often has) overcome the former, Levinas holds that these need not be mutually exclusive.[17]

Said (le Dit)

Another central term associated with wisdom is 'said' (*le Dit*), used with greatest frequency in *Otherwise than Being*. In Levinas's theory of language, 'said' is contrasted with 'saying' (*le Dire*) and where saying is associated with subjectivity, said is associated with objectivity. Ontology, of which Levinas is so critical, begins with the said: "The birthplace of ontology is in the said" (OB, 42). Levinas writes that in "language *qua* said everything is conveyed before us" (OB, 6). The said is that which is written, displayed, formalized in the structures and systems of language. It is in "the structure of the said, in which identical entities, beings, are shown" (OB, 38). The 'saying' is that out of which the 'said' emerges, but the said is incapable of exhaustively capturing the saying, as is seen when Levinas writes, "[t]he said and the non-said do not absorb all the saying, which remains on this side of, or goes beyond, the said" (OB, 23). One of the clearest descriptions of the said is found in a later work, when Levinas asks, "Is language meaningful only in its *said*, in its propositions in the indicative, everywhere at least latent, in the theoretical content of affirmed or virtual judgments, in pure communication of information—in its said, in all that can be written?" (DR, 164; my emphasis).

By contrast, the saying is that of language which cannot be written. He writes that saying is "my exposure without reserve to the other" (OB, 168). Though the saying and said are understood as contrasting terms, these terms, like many of the opposing pairs of terms already observed, are not mutually exclusive.[18]

Though the said can be described as "that which can be written," that does not make the distinction between said and saying one of 'written' and 'spoken.' Rather, even that which is spoken is the said rather than saying. In fact, 'speech' (*parole*) is another term associated with the discourse of the said as when Levinas links speech with 'philosophical discourse' (OB, 169). He defines speech as follows: "Speech, then, is a relationship between freedoms who neither limit nor deny one another, but reciprocally affirm one another" (IT, 35). Speech, then, is a term that describes a type of said which is not totalizing, and is marked by a respectful, nonreductive reciprocity.

A distinguishing mark of the said is the establishment of a 'proposition.' Levinas writes, "the one-for-the-other . . . states the idealized *said*. . . . *Judgments* and propositions are born in *justice*, which is putting together, assembling the being of entities" (OB, 161; my emphasis). The "said remains a proposition" and "[b]eing, the verb of a proposition, is to be sure, a theme" (OB, 47).

Thematization (la Thématisation)

Thus, the said is closely linked to the next subset of terms related to wisdom: 'theme,' 'thematization,' 'thought,' 'reason,' 'consciousness,' 'knowledge,' 'intelligence,' and 'intentionality.' Levinas writes that "[t]hought, intelligence, mind and psyche would appear to be consciousness, or on the threshold of consciousness." He continues, saying that "Human consciousness would be their perfected modality: the consciousness of an *I identical* in its *I* think, aiming at and embracing, or perceiving, all alterity under its thematizing gaze. This aiming of thought is called intentionality" (DR, 159; my emphasis).

'Thematization' (*thématisation*) risks eliminating difference since it is the act of finding what is the same. The thematizing gaze seeks a reduction to that which is identical. "Philosophy serves justice by thematizing the difference" (OB, 165), but this thematizing need not become final or absolute since philosophy also serves justice by "reducing the thematized to difference" (OB, 165). The Other is 'non-thematizable' (OB, 12, 77), but there is nonetheless a way to make a theme of the Other without doing so absolutely, as we shall see in later chapters.[19]

'Thought' [*pensée*] is closely related to thematization as revealed when Levinas writes that "thought aims at themes" (OB, 46). So here again, as with so many of these terms, thought could mistakenly be taken as that which should always be avoided, since thought is what aims at themes—eliminating the differences of the Other. But there is nonetheless a type of "[t]hought that is not an adequation to the other, for whom I can no longer be the measure" (DR, 168). This nontotalizing thought may seek to make a theme of the Other by taking measurements and making comparisons, but it nonetheless recognizes that the Other's "uniqueness is refractory to every measure" (DR, 168).

'Reason' (*la raison*) is like thought in its association with thematization. Reason is the faculty which thematizes, and there is a "reason [that is] characteristic of . . . thematization" (OB, 167). Levinas is critical of reason, but more specifically, he is critical of reason that completely absorbs the difference of the Other. If reason always destroyed the difference of the Other in this way, then there would be no positive forms of reason for Levinas, but he does not make this claim. In fact, in response to the question of whether or not reason "succeed[s] in absorbing into its coherence the intelligibility of proximity [of the Other]," he replies, "Does not the latter [that is, the difference of the Other] have to be subordinated to the former [that is, reason]?" (OB, 167). In order to avoid reason absorbing the Other, reason must be subordinated to the responsibility of the Other rather than vice versa. Rather than deducing responsibility from reason, reason must be recognized as coming out of the original responsibility. "The love of one's fellowman, and his original right, as unique and incomparable, for which I am answerable, tend of their own accord to make appeal to a Reason capable of comparing incomparables, a wisdom of love" (UN, 195). As mentioned above in the discussion of the third, when the relation with the Other encounters a third, "[t]he relation with the other and the unique . . . comes to require a reason that thematizes" (PP, 142).

Also in the group of terms associated with thematization is 'consciousness' (*conscience*). "And this thematization of saying does indeed bring out in
it the characteristics of consciousness" (OB, 46). This consciousness is
understood as intentionality. "Thought, intelligence, mind, and psyche
would appear to be consciousness, or on the threshold of consciousness.
Human consciousness would be their perfected modality: the consciousness
of an *I identical* in its *I think*, aiming at and embracing, or perceiving all
alterity under its thematizing gaze. This aiming of thought is called intentionality" (DR, 159; emphasis in the original). And like many of the terms
in this section, 'consciousness' is born in the presence of the third.
"Consciousness is born as the presence of the third party in the proximity of
the one to the other" (PP, 144). And like the previous terms discussed,
Levinas's critique of consciousness simply critiques the way philosophy has
often misplaced it as founding goodness and ethics rather than the other way
around. Consciousness is entirely permissible, even required for justice, just
so long as it is understood that it is derived from goodness, not vice versa.
"[I]t is not consciousness that establishes the Good, but the Good which
calls forth consciousness" (DTO, 204).

Likewise, even though Levinas generally rejects 'knowledge' as totalitarian and reductive, he is not opposed to it *simpliciter*. Knowledge of
which he is critical is a "return to presence, that is to say, to being" and it is
a "comprehended presence." Knowledge, in this sense, is defined as the
"assembly of those ideas, to their synthesis, to the unity of their appercep-
tion, to the com-prehension" (FOO, 136). Even though he generally rejects
this unity-seeking, difference-eliminating knowledge, he speaks of a right
time for knowledge. Even though the relationship to the Other is "irreducible to knowledge . . . it may eventually call for knowledge, faced with
others in the plural, a knowledge required by justice" (DR, 168). In either
case, knowledge is related to being: "In knowledge, there is a relation to
presence, that is to say, to being; in ontology . . . the structures . . . of union
reappear" (FOO, 137). And it is to this terminology of ontology and being
to which I now turn.

Ontology (*l'Ontologie*)

It would be difficult to understand this family of wisdom terms without
understanding how Levinas uses the terms 'ontology' and 'being,' since they
are so frequently and uniquely used. For Levinas, ontology does not just refer
to theories of being, but he is speaking of the epistemology of being, as in
Husserlian and Heideggerian ontologies. Levinas writes that "*Being and*

Time has argued perhaps but one sole thesis: Being is inseparable from the comprehension of Being (which unfolds as time)" (TI, 45).

We repeatedly find this use of ontology to mean the "comprehension of being" (TI, 45, 47; OB, 155). However, just because the critique begins with Husserl and Heidegger does not mean that it ends there; in fact, once we understand that ontology is construed as 'comprehension' or 'conceptualization,' it then becomes applicable to much of philosophy in the Western tradition. This wide scope is seen when Levinas writes, "Western philosophy has most often been an ontology: a reduction of the other to the same by interposition of a middle and neutral term that ensures the comprehension of being" (TI, 43).

In addition to the most succinct definition of ontology as the "comprehension of being," ontology is also described as 'cognition' (TI, 43), 'conceptualization' (TI, 46), 'embracing of Being' (TI, 47), 'grasping' the existent, conceptual 'possession' (TI, 46), 'reduction,' and "neutralization of the other who becomes a theme or an object" (TI, 43).

Politics (la Politique)

Finally, among all the terms associated with wisdom, this last set refers to the most formalized and systematized forms of wisdom and includes such terms as 'politics,' 'the state,' 'institutions,' 'legislation,' and 'philosophy.'

This final set of terms arises out of 'the third,' which requires comparison, which requires predication and thought which are understood ontologically, and which require formalization and the regulation by law and the delivery of the law in the form of politics and philosophy. This complex relationship is expressed as follows: "All the attributes of individual beings, of entities that are fixed in or by nouns, as predicates can be understood as modes of being; such are the qualities of which the entities make a show, the typical generalities by which they are ordered, the laws that regulate them, the logical forms that contain and deliver them" (OB, 41). Precisely because this last set of terms is the most systematized and furthest removed from the relationship between I and the Other, Levinas uses these terms in a disparaging way more often than he does the other wisdom-related terms. For example, he speaks of the "State, which, [sic] violently excludes subversive discourse" (OB, 170) and a "State in which the interpersonal relationship is impossible, in which it is directed in advance by the determinism proper to the state" (PJL, 105). Furthermore, "[p]olitics, left to itself, has its own determinism" (PJL, 108). This determinism of the state and politics is one that by necessity ends in totalitarianism. However, despite his strong language in opposition to many instantiations of the state and politics, even these are not rejected completely. The qualification is important when he says that politics, *left to itself*, leads to totalitarianism.

The terms 'law' (*la Loi*) and 'legislation' (*la Législation*) are also associated with the term politics but take on an even greater degree of systemization. The law is what results when the 'saying' becomes 'said.' "The saying is fixed in a said, is written, becomes a book, law and science" (OB, 159). But what more can be said about Levinas's understanding of law besides the writing or systematizing of politics and wisdom? He describes the definitional function of law as that which regulates the pursuit of symmetry and equality. The asymmetry of my infinite obligation to the Other will eventually seek a symmetry when the third arrives, and this pursuit of symmetry eventually becomes formulated and regulated by law. "Whatever be the ways that lead to the superstructure of society, in justice, the dissymmetry that holds me at odds with regard to the other will find again law, autonomy, equality" (OB, 127). This law is necessary and often takes forms which harm the Other, but even this term law can be associated with wisdom of love if properly qualified.

Finally, I will mention the term 'philosophy' (*philosophie*) which Levinas also uses in association with the terms in this section. Like law, which is a formalization of the pursuit of justice, 'philosophy' is an ordered form of measuring the infinite responsibility for the Other. "To the extravagant generosity of the for-the-other is superposed a reasonable, ancillary or angelic order; that of justice through knowledge and here philosophy is a measure brought to the infinite of the being-for-the-other of peace and proximity, and as it were a wisdom of love" (PP, 144).

Even though philosophy is an order and measurement of the infinite, it also serves to remind us of the immeasurability of that which it measures. A philosophy that is not inherently totalitarian recognizes its own limitations and the impossibility of complete certainty. "Philosophy is called upon to conceive ambivalence" (OB, 162). For philosophy to be a 'wisdom of love,' it must remain subservient to that to which it is bringing order. The order must not dominate that out of which it arises, but even "if it is called to thought by justice, it still synchronizes in the said the diachrony of the difference between the one and the other, and remains the servant of the saying that signifies the difference between the one and the other as the one for the other, as non-indifference to the other. Philosophy is the wisdom of love at the service of love" (OB, 162). So philosophy, if properly serving love, is not rejected out of hand, but we will need to examine more closely (in chapter 4) the way in which philosophy is to be in the service of love.

I have just clustered the extensive Levinasian nomenclature on wisdom around the following terms: 'justice,' 'comparison,' 'the said,' 'thematization,' 'ontology,' and 'politics.' Before 'the third' is present, these terms are used critically and refer to the negative love of wisdom. The way in which the third makes wisdom necessary will be treated in chapters 3 and 4, but I will note here that it is a crucial distinction because when there is no third, wisdom is always violent, yet when the third is present, wisdom becomes necessary, and this necessary wisdom can be (but is not always) pacific. Even though some of these groups of terms rarely are found being used referring to wisdom of love, such as 'ontology,' and 'thematization,' most of the terms, with the proper qualification, avoid Levinas's universal dismissal.

Although a full treatment of the difference between the love of wisdom and the wisdom of love will be provided in later chapters, I will point to a few terminological cues that will help us discern the two types of wisdom.

Wisdom Terminology: Anonymous Wisdom

Although most of the terms used above can be used to refer either to the love of wisdom (which he criticizes) or the wisdom of love (which he endorses), there is one term that is never used in a positive context—and that is 'anonymous wisdom.' Another term never used to describe wisdom of love is 'totalitarian,' and a third term used to describe the sort of wisdom he critiques is 'originally antagonistic.' While the term 'totalitarian' refers to the telos of this type of wisdom, and 'originally antagonistic' refers to its origin, 'anonymous' describes the means with which this wisdom is carried out.[20]

Anonymous

The term 'anonymous' is used often, and in every case it refers to that which is opposed to the wisdom of love. Once wisdom, justice, and politics become necessary, Levinas warns that "justice, society and truth itself which they require, must not be taken for an anonymous law of the 'human forces' governing an impersonal totality" (OB, 161). By anonymous, he means that it is a legality that makes judgments without seeing the person. The anonymous law is one that is administered without a face—judgment without a judge. "What is inhuman is to be judged without anyone who judges" (IT, 31). And as this justice has no face, it also ignores the face of the one it judges, which makes it depersonalizing.

This depersonalizing wisdom is a philosophy or political justice which prevents "the face of the other from being recognized" (VF, 176). The central flaw of this form of justice is that it ignores the uniqueness of the individual face. In organizing the state "according to abstract rules, and in the name of anonymous powers" (US, 114), the face of the unique Other is not seen. It is impartiality taken to such an extreme that it completely reduces the Other to cases under a genre as is the case of a "State . . . with the simple subsuming of cases beneath the general rule, as the computer is capable of doing" (PP, 144). This pure calculation defaces and is causally connected to the rise of totalitarianism. When justice does not recognize the unique face of the other, but sees the human being it administers as "anonymous individuality . . . [it] runs the risk of totalitarianism" (VF, 176).

Totalitarian

That the *telos* of this anonymous, impersonal wisdom is totalitarian is seen when Levinas writes that the "state in which the interpersonal relationship is impossible, in which it is directed in advance by the determinism proper to the state, is a *totalitarian state*" (PJL, 105; my emphasis). This state exists for its own sake alone. Although not each institution or political structure is guilty of making itself its own totality and end, it is precisely this feature which he strictly critiques, warning that "being,[21] totality, the State, politics,[22] techniques, work, are at every moment on the point of having their center of gravitation in themselves, and weighing on their own account" (OB, 159).

By the time a State exists solely for itself and thus becomes totalitarian, it may be easy to see how this type of anonymous wisdom is not a wisdom of love; Levinas tries to draw attention to the source of this totalitarian politics, and we often see him doing so by referring to terminology of origins. As we shall see in greater depth in later chapters, Levinas traces totalitarian, anonymous, defacing wisdom to a misunderstanding of the origin of wisdom and politics.

When anonymous judgment ignores the face of the Other and forgets the uniqueness of the one whom the law judges, it is forgetting the true origin of judgment. When the law "forgets that [origin], it risks sinking into a totalitarian and Stalinist regime" (OUJ, 230). This direct causality is underscored when Levinas writes that "the forgetfulness of [the origin of justice] risks transforming the sublime and difficult work of justice[23] into a purely political calculation—to the point of totalitarian abuse" (VF, 170).

Originally Antagonistic

Thus, we should be alert to terminology of origins, since wisdom, which traces its source to 'original antagonism' as Hobbes[24] would have it, is in danger of totalitarianism. Levinas cautions against this "anonymous legality regulating human masses, from which a technique of social equilibrium has been derived to harmonize antagonistic, blind forces through transitional cruelty and violence" (PP, 143).

It is understandable why some think that Levinas is dismissing politics categorically, when he writes that the "state, institutions and even the courts . . . expose themselves essentially to an eventually inhuman but characteristic determinism—politics" (DR, 165). But he shows otherwise by noting that we can avoid this "determinism by 'going back to [politics'] motivation in justice and a foundational inter-humanity" (DR, 165). The central difference here between politics that become totalitarian and politics that do not become so is found in the awareness of the *origin* of politics. The non-totalitarian state's "imperative motivation is inscribed in the very right of the other man, unique and incomparable" (UN, 196).

Levinas rejects politics that sees its origin in "antagonistic forces" (OB, 159). Thus, politics, which are understood as proceeding from a Hobbesian "clash of all against all" (OB, 4), is never a wisdom of love. The way in which one views the origins of justice has significant consequences for the way in which that justice is carried out.

Despite the criticism Levinas has for forms of wisdom that 1) originate in antagonistic, self-interested forces, 2) serve the state as an end unto itself, and 3) are anonymously administered, these characteristics do not exhaust all possible forms of wisdom. It is to this alternative wisdom that I now turn—the wisdom Levinas calls a 'wisdom of love' (*sagesse d'l'amour*).

Wisdom Terminology: Wisdom of Love

In clarifying the terminology associated with the wisdom of love, it is important to note that many of the terms Levinas uses to describe the anonymous 'love of wisdom' mentioned above are also used to describe its alternative— the 'wisdom of love.' This can be confusing, since one could conclude by his use of the terms in the critical way described earlier, that he is critical of wisdom in all of its forms. However, in various texts, Levinas consistently shows that most of the terms mentioned above are also, if appropriately qualified, used in association with wisdom of love—the type of wisdom he endorses. First, I will show that these terms are indeed linked to wisdom of love, and then I will identify some of the key terminological phrases used to qualify wisdom as wisdom of love.

In *Otherwise than Being*, we see how these many terms[25] are linked with each other and with wisdom of love:

> The extraordinary commitment of the other to the third party calls for control, a search for justice, society and the State, *comparison* and possession, *thought* and science, commerce and *philosophy*, and outside of anarchy, the search for a *principle*. Philosophy is this *measure* brought to the infinity of the being-for-the-other of proximity, and is like the *wisdom* of love. (OB, 161)

Showing further evidence of the interweaving of these terms, culminating in the wisdom of love are two long but important excerpts. It is important to see how these terms are intertwined in a sustained, unbroken weaving of nomenclature. The first example is from "Philosophy, Justice, and Love":

> I don't live in a world in which there is but one single 'first comer'; there is always a third party in the world: he or she is also my other, my fellow. Hence, it is important to me to know which of the two takes precedence. Is the one not the persecutor of the other? Must not human beings, who are incomparable, be compared? Thus justice, here, takes precedence over the taking upon oneself of the fate of the other. I must *judge*, where before I was to assume responsibilities. Here is the birth of the *theoretical*; here the concern for justice is born, which is the basis of the theoretical. . . . At a certain moment, there is a necessity for a '*weighing*,' a *comparison*, a *pondering*, and in this sense philosophy would be the appearance of *wisdom* from the depths of that initial charity; it would be—and I am not playing on words—the *wisdom* of that charity the *wisdom* of love. (PJL, 104)

In another example from "Peace and Proximity," we see a similarly large group of 'wisdom' terms all linked in a way that culminates in the phrase wisdom of love. Levinas writes:

> The *third* party is . . . [the birth] of the question. The first question . . . is the question of *justice*. Henceforth it becomes necessary to know, to make oneself a *conscience*. To my relation with the unique and the incomparable, comparison is superimposed, and, with a view to equity or equality, a *weighing*, a *calculation*, the *comparison* of incomparables . . . presence or *representation*—of *being*, the *thematization* and visibility of the face, discountenanced in a manner of speaking as the simple individuation of the individual; the *weight* of having and of exchanges; the necessity of thinking together beneath one synthetic theme the multiple and the unity of the

world; and thereby the promotion of the relation and ultimate signifying-ness of *being* to intentional and intelligible *thought*; and finally thereby the extreme importance in human multiplicity of the *political* structure of society under the rule of *law*, and hence *institutions* in which the *for-the-other* of subjectivity—in which the I enters with the dignity of the citizen in to the perfect reciprocity of political laws that are essentially egalitarian or held to become so. (PP, 143; my emphasis)

Levinas concludes this line of thought saying that "here philosophy is a *measure* brought to the infinite of the being-for-the-other of peace and proximity, and as it were a wisdom of love" (PP, 144; my emphasis).

These are three of the most terminologically concentrated passages related to the wisdom of love; there are others, however, which also underscore these connections.[26] The movement is from the Other to the third, which requires justice, which requires comparison, which is accomplished through predication (said) and thematization which is understood as ontology and is formulated and systematized as philosophy and politics which establish laws to regulate justice and institutions to implement the laws.

The terminology we see describing this wisdom of love is 'watchfulness of persons,' in contrast to an 'anonymous' observation, 'concern-for-the third,' in contrast to concern for the 'totalitarian' state, and 'original responsibility' in contrast to 'original antagonism.'

Watchfulness of Persons

In contrast to a wisdom that is administered anonymously, wisdom of love is carried out face-to-face. The judgments made by a wisdom of love are those that are made by persons who see persons, not by absolute calculations. The term that best captures this quality of the wisdom of love is a 'watchfulness of persons.' In order to avoid a State that becomes "abandoned to its necessity," the wisdom of love "ceaselessly calls for the watchfulness of persons, who cannot content themselves with the simple subsuming of cases beneath the general rule, as the computer is capable of doing" (PP, 144). It is true that justice and politics are necessary after the third arrives, but this justice must be watched by persons, not mere rules. In fact, "Love must always watch over justice" (PJL, 108). Justice that is not watched by particular persons in relation to particular Others is a justice which has no oversight, but the "institutions that justice requires must be subject to the oversight of charity" (VF, 176).

Concern-for-the-third

If the watchfulness of persons is to be the *means* for the wisdom of love, then the 'concern-for-the-third' is to be the *telos* of the wisdom of love. While an anonymously administered wisdom is in ultimate service to the state, wisdom of love seeks to take the third into consideration without forgetting about the Other.

Infinite responsibility for the Other exists before the third arrives, but Levinas claims that "to this idea—without contradicting it—I immediately add the concern for the third and hence, justice" (PJL, 105). The difference between the state operating with the wisdom of love and the state seeking its own totality is that the former can be limited. The state that serves itself rather than the third "is a state in which the interpersonal relationship is impossible" (PJL, 105).

Original Responsibility

Perhaps the most distinguishing feature of the wisdom of love, however, is its genealogy. The totalitarian anonymous wisdom emerges from a wisdom that views itself as harmonizing antagonistic forces. Levinas's wisdom of love, however, recognizes the fact that wisdom began in original responsibility for the Other. As I will show, not all law is rejected—law can be good, but this goodness comes from understanding how it arose. The 'good law' is law that remembers that "it is not as just as the kindness that instigates it is good" (OUJ, 230). And it is vital to know that the egalitarian state proceeds from the "irreducible responsibility for the Other" (PP, 144). If Hobbes was right, then the original human drive is one of selfish violence, and the "state emerges from . . . the limitation of violence—one cannot set a limit[27] on the state" (PJL, 105). This wisdom of love, however, recognizes that the human begins in original responsibility for the Other and that the state emerges out of "the limitation of charity" (PJL, 105). How these views of wisdom's origin differ and how this makes a difference will be treated in chapter 5.

In sum of the terminology used to distinguish these two types of wisdom, philosophy at its best remembers its origin (arising out of concern for the third) and it remembers that it is not final. "The fact that the other, my neighbor is also a third party with respect to another . . . is the birth of . . . philosophy. The unlimited initial responsibility, which justifies . . . philosophy can be forgotten. In this forgetting consciousness is a pure egoism. But egoism is neither first nor last" (OB, 128). So, philosophy at its best knows that it is does not arise in the first instance for the self; it also knows that, in the end, it is not ultimately for the self; and the means for administering this wisdom of love is a 'watchfulness of persons.'

§2 'Love' (*l'amour*) Terminology

'Love' Terminology in General

Now I turn to the second of two major sets of terms in Levinas's work— namely, the family of terms roughly associated with the term 'love.' I am hesitant to use the term love, as Levinas was, due to its lack of precision. Especially in his earlier works, Levinas often avoided the unqualified use of the term love,[28] and in explaining why, he wrote, "the word love, it is a worn-out and ambiguous word" (PJL, 108). It is especially missing from *Totality and Infinity*, which he explains as follows: "In *Totality and Infinity* I do not use the word 'love' because by love is often understood what Pascal called love with concupiscence" (PL, 174).

Nonetheless, it is precisely the word's lack of precision that makes it useful here, since it is broad enough to include two important subsets of terms—one set which includes the terms 'desire,' '*agape*,' and 'love without concupiscence'; the other set includes the terms 'need,' '*eros*,' and 'concupiscence.' In this section I will identify the sets of terms Levinas associates with each type of love, show the subgroupings of terms, and provide texts that define or come close to defining each term.

The terms which can be grouped with 'need' include '*eros*,' 'hunger,' 'void,' the 'for-itself,' 'egoism,' 'separation,' 'interiority,' 'concupiscence,' 'satiation,' 'enjoyment,' 'sensibility,' 'consumption,' 'satisfaction,' 'possession,' and 'living from.' That Levinas viewed these terms as linked is seen in the following: "To be me . . . at home with oneself, separated . . . these are synonyms. Egoism, enjoyment, sensibility, and the whole dimension of interiority [are] articulations of separation" (TI, 148). Some of these interlinking terms are, as Levinas says, synonyms, but some of the terms are 'articulations' of some of these synonyms, and I will address the ways that these different terms give similar but unique expression of need.

The terms which can be grouped with 'desire' are far more in number and include '*agape*,' 'metaphysical desire,' 'exteriority,' 'love without concupiscence,' 'love without *eros*,' 'love of one's neighbor,' 'ethical relation,' 'conscience,' 'infinity,' 'authority,' 'saying,' 'disinterestedness,' 'responsibility,' 'revelation,' 'holiness,' 'call,' 'accusation,' 'substitution,' 'incarnation,' 'suffering,' 'sacrifice,' 'hostage,' 'persecution,' 'obsession,' 'trauma,' 'host,' 'welcome,' 'genuine freedom,' 'independence,' 'here I am,' 'attraction,' 'aspiration,' 'marvel,' 'goodness,' 'care,' and 'grace.' Again, these are not a simple list of synonyms, since some of these words share more in common than others, which I will explain, but each of them emphasizes some unique feature of desire which no one term or definition could completely capture.

I will unfold some of the unique distinguishing qualities in these various terms and I will also argue that the most prominent distinction Levinas makes between need and desire is described in terms of satiability and a-satiability. I am suggesting that the key feature of need, as Levinas uses the term, is *satiable* desire. I am also suggesting that the key feature of desire— seen in contrast to need—is the fact that it is *a-satiable*. Thus the entire set of terms related to need include some quality of satiability, while the entire set of terms involved with desire is such that it is neither satiable nor insatiable, but entirely outside of the concept of satiation. This distinction can be seen when Levinas writes that "the difference between need and Desire [is that] in need I can sink my teeth into the real and satisfy myself in assimilating the other; in Desire there is no sinking one's teeth into being" (TI, 117). It is easy to think that desire—especially when he calls it 'insatiable desire'—is merely an unfulfilled need. But he directly clarifies that confusion when he writes, "Desire does not coincide with an unsatisfied need; it is situated beyond satisfaction and non-satisfaction" (TI, 179).

I grant that understanding Levinas's distinction between the two types of love in terms of satiable desire and a-satiable desire may not be immediately obvious for two reasons: first, Levinas used unconventional terminology[29] in making these distinctions. Secondly, the very idea of an a-satiable desire may seem like an oxymoron if one presupposes that all desire arises out of a lack and seeks satiation. It is a goal of this section to address the first of these two problems by clarifying the technical and unconventional terminology. Doing so will make it more obvious that Levinas is indeed arguing for the possibility of an a-satiable desire that is not reducible to satiable desire. I will address the second problem—arguing for the plausibility of an a-satiable desire—in chapter 5.

'Love' Terminology: Need (Satiable Desire)

The terms for 'need' listed above all relate to satiability, and there are at least three major features of satiability to which Levinas draws our attention. The first is that satiable desire comes from a state of lack. The second is that satiable desire is initiated by the subject who seeks to be filled, and the third feature of satiable desire is that it is capable of being satiated, even if only partially or temporarily. Some of the terms Levinas uses (like 'need') capture all of these features while others emphasize one of the features. He says that 'need' (*besoin*) proceeds from lack, and that need has the *capacity* for satiation—if only in part or in degrees.

Again and again, we see Levinas pointing to the privative nature of need. "Need, a happy dependence, is capable of satisfaction, like a void, which gets filled" (TI, 115). Several terms associated with need also emphasize the privative quality of satiable desire, including 'void,' 'lack,' 'hunger,' and 'privation.' Satiable desire is spoken of as a 'void' (OB, 73), which could apply to one's appetites (OB, 73) or to the soul (TI, 62). Levinas says that "need is a lack [*un manque*]" (TI, 115) or that the need proceeds from a 'lack' (TI, 33, 269, 299; MS, 51). This 'lacking' or empty quality of satiable desire is sometimes referred to in terms of hunger. The egoist is without ears for the Other, and is "like a hungry stomach" (TI, 134). The hunger terminology is used not only to refer to the corporeal hunger (OB, 77) but also to cognitive hunger that he calls the "[t]he emptiness of hunger" (OB, 72) or a "certain negativity . . . like a hunger [*une faim*]" (OB, 96). And again, in a more summary fashion, we read that "Hunger is need, is privation in the primal sense of the word" (TI, 111). These are various ways of describing the "privation [*la privation*] of need" (TI, 115), but Levinas's analysis of need is not completed merely in terms of noting privation or lack. This lack also seeks satisfaction.

The second important fact to mention, then, about satiable desire is that the self *initiates* the pursuit of filling the lack. It originates in the ego, and "proceeds from the subject" (TI, 62). One term that draws attention to this satisfaction-seeking quality of satiable desire is the 'for itself' (*pour soi*). The 'for itself' or 'for oneself' expresses the egoistic, self-seeking nature of satiable desire (OB, 50, 52; MS, 51). It brings into focus the role of one's will over which one has control. "The *for itself* in consciousness is thus the very power which a being exercises upon itself, its will, its sovereignty" (OB, 102). In using the term 'for itself' Levinas emphasizes not only a seeking and an exercise of power, but the fact that the self is the one who is an initiator. The pursuit of satiation is a matter of "initiative and power" (TI, 51). This 'initiation' and self-causing (*sui causa*) are key elements of satiable desire, and are also expressed in terms of 'egoism' (*l'égoïsme*), which is described by Levinas as the "source of the will" (TI, 59) that has a will which seeks to satisfy itself. But this ego-seeking satisfaction does not exhaust the concept of satiable desire; this leads us to the third feature of satiable desire, which is that the ego is also capable of finding what it seeks.

Finally and importantly, I will note that this satiable desire is not merely a privation that seeks and does not find. Rather, this is a desire that can be satiated, even if only temporarily. Levinas's analysis of needs is such that they are "capable of being satisfied" (TI, 117). In contrast to "simple privation" as Plato analyzes need, which has need as a state of unhappy, impoverished emptiness, Levinas suggests that we no longer "remain at a philosophy of need that apprehends it in poverty" (TI, 116). Instead, it is a happy privation, since it is a privation capable of being satiated. "For the privation of need is not just a privation, but is privation in a being that knows the surplus of happiness, privation in a being gratified" (TI, 115). Additional terms which emphasize this capacity for satiation include 'enjoyment,' 'separation,' 'interiority,' 'satisfaction,' 'consumption,' 'possession,' 'living from,' and 'being at home.' The interconnection of these terms is shown when Levinas writes, "Egoism is life: life from . . . or enjoyment" that occurs "in the interiority of being at home with oneself, and hence labor and possession" (TI, 175).

'Enjoyment' is the happy state arising from the satisfaction of need, but it is not destroyed by the pain or emptiness of need. The "happiness of enjoyment, [is] a satisfaction of needs which is not compromised by the need-satisfaction rhythm" (TI, 144). In fact, the "happiness of enjoyment flourishes on the 'pain' of need" since it is the emptiness that allows for the pleasure of the filling. Satiable desire includes the ability to be satiated, but also includes that desire when it is not yet satisfied. Enjoyment is in fact "experienced as limited" since it is "not ensured against the unknown that lurks in the very element it enjoys" (TI, 144). So this enjoyment is capable of satiation, even though limited in its capacity for complete and final satiability, and it is crucial to note this fact about satiable desire, since it helps clarify what he means by the term 'insatiable desire' that he contrasts with satiable desire.[30] Similar to enjoyment[31] is the term 'possession' because it marks the actual satisfaction of the ego. But the two terms are not merely synonymous, and Levinas points to the difference by saying that "[p]ossession proceeding from the dwelling is to be distinguished from the content possessed and the enjoyment of that content" (TI, 158). Though both 'enjoyment' and 'possession' denote a satiation of the ego, possession further implies that the ego has taken and grasped this satisfaction. "Possession is accomplished in taking possession . . . the destiny of the hand. The hand is the organ of grasping and taking" (TI, 159). This possession can be a possession of the "bread I eat, the land in which I dwell, the landscape I contemplate" or even the Other. Emphasizing the fact that this desire can be satiated, Levinas continues, "I can 'feed' on these realities and to a very great extent satisfy myself, as though I had simply been lacking them" (TI, 33). That the ego attempts to possess the Other will be of great concern.

"Possession is preeminently the form in which the other becomes the same, by becoming mine" (TI, 46).

Thus, satiable desire, expressed in these many different ways, proceeds from a lack, is self-initiated, and has at least some capacity for satiation. These features of satiable desire are in contrast to a-satiable desire, which does not come from privation, is not self-initiated and is not capable of satiation, as we shall see.

'Love' Terminology: Desire (A-satiable Desire)

In addition to speaking of love in terms of satiable desire (as we have just examined), Levinas also speaks of another type of love. The variety of terms used to describe this alternative love is wide, and it includes the following: 'metaphysical desire,' 'exteriority,' 'love without concupiscence,' 'love without *eros*,' '*agape*,' 'love of one's neighbor,' 'ethics,' 'ethical relation,' 'conscience,' 'infinity,' 'authority,' 'saying,' 'disinterestedness,' 'responsibility,' 'revelation,' 'holiness,' 'call,' 'accusation,' 'substitution,' 'incarnation,' 'suffering,' 'sacrifice,' 'hostage,' 'persecution,' 'obsession,' 'trauma,' 'host,' 'welcome,' 'genuine freedom,' 'independence,' 'here I am,' 'attraction,' 'aspiration,' 'marvel,' 'goodness,' 'care,' 'grace,' and 'insatiable desire.' When he uses the unmodified term 'desire,' it is referring to the insatiable or a-satiable desire. Although some of these terms are used more frequently in certain texts than in others, I will argue that there is more continuity between these various works (and the terms therein) than there is discontinuity.

In *Totality and Infinity* (1961/1969), the most frequently used terms for a-satiable desire are 'desire' and 'metaphysical desire.' Desire is closely linked with the term 'metaphysics': "We have posited metaphysics as Desire. We have described Desire as the 'measure' of the infinite which . . . no satisfaction arrests" (TI, 304). Metaphysics, in turn, is linked with several other terms or phrases such as 'transcendence,' 'welcoming' or 'calling into question,' and 'ethics.' "Metaphysics, transcendence, the welcoming of the other by the same . . . is concretely produced as the calling into question of the same by the other, that is, as . . . ethics" (TI, 43). Levinas also associates desire with the 'infinite' and with 'disinterestedness,' and with 'goodness,' as is seen when he writes of "the Desire for the Infinite which the desirable arouses rather than satisfies. A Desire perfectly disinterested—goodness" (TI, 50). Desire is linked to goodness and being when he "posit[s] being as Desire and as goodness" (TI, 305). 'Being,' in turn, is linked to exteriority: "Being is exteriority" (TI, 290). And exteriority is linked to several other terms, including 'alterity,' 'the appeal (or call) of the other,' and 'marvel.' Continuing the chain of terms, 'exteriority' is nearly interchangeable with several other terms, such as 'alterity,' 'appeal,' and 'marvel,' as is seen in these excerpts: "Exteriority, or, if one prefers, alterity" (TI, 290); "[h]is exteriority, that is, his appeal to me" (TI, 291); and "[e]xteriority is . . . a marvel" (TI, 292).

In *Otherwise than Being* (1974/1981), Levinas's nomenclature shifts somewhat, and phrases and terms emphasizing one's hostile obligation to the Other become ubiquitous—phrases such as 'responsibility for the Other,' 'for the Other,' and the term 'substitution' are among the most frequently used. Substitution and responsibility for the Other are related to each other and to 'hostage' and 'accusation' in many places, including when Levinas writes, "for under accusation by everyone, the responsibility for everyone goes to the point of substitution. A subject is hostage" (OB, 112). Accusation is associated with several other terms, including 'passivity,' 'persecution,' and 'expiation': "This accusation can be reduced to the passivity of the self only as a persecution, but a persecution that turns into an expiation" (OB, 112). Passivity, in turn, can be seen linked with 'subjectivity' and 'obsession': "The most passive, unassumable, passivity, the subjectivity or the very subjection of the subject, is due to my being obsessed with responsibility for the oppressed who is other than myself" (OB, 55). And in an ambitious clustering of these terms, Levinas draws explicit attention to the interrelatedness of his use of these and additional terms. He writes:

> Vulnerability, exposure to outrage, to wounding, passivity more passive than all patience, passivity of the accusative form, trauma of accusation suffered by a hostage to the point of persecution, implicating the identity of the hostage who substitutes himself for the others: all this is the self, a defecting or defeat of the ego's identity. And this, pushed to the limit, is sensibility, sensibility as the subjectivity of the subject. It is a substitution for another, one in place of another, expiation. (OB, 15)

And he continues this string of terms writing, "[s]ubstitution, at the limit of being, ends up in saying[32] [*le Dire*]" (OB, 15).

In the later essays found in *Entre Nous* (1991/1998), there appears to be another terminological shift as Levinas less frequently uses the harsh terms so frequent in *Otherwise than Being* like 'substitution' and 'hostage' but continues to use the phrase 'responsibility for the Other.' Even though Levinas admits, "I don't very much like the word love, which is worn-out and debased" (PJL, 103), he uses it in several phrases which begin appearing quite often such as 'love without concupiscence,' 'love without *eros*,' 'love of one's neighbor,' and '*agape*.'[33] We can see Levinas demonstrating that these terms are closely related when he writes, "the responsibility for my neighbor, which is, no doubt, the harsh name for what we call love of one's neighbor; love without *Eros*, charity, love in which the ethical aspect dominates the passionate aspect, love without concupiscence" (PJL, 103). And he views "Agape in terms of responsibility for the other" (PJL, 113). Other associated phrases include 'love without reciprocity,' 'here I am,' 'gratuitousness,' 'grace,' and 'unconditional charity'—all of which are linked when Levinas speaks of "love without concupiscence [which] . . . is in its 'here I am' of an I, in its noninterchangeable uniqueness of one chosen. It is originally without reciprocity, which would risk compromising its gratuitousness or grace or unconditional charity" (OUJ, 228–29).

Although these word clusters from early, middle, and late texts seem to imply a change in thought, I am suggesting that there is greater continuity in his thought than the change in terminology suggests. First, I should point out that while certain terms occur with greater frequency in certain texts, most of these terms can be found throughout the earlier, middle, and later works. For example, although terms such as 'desire' and 'metaphysical desire' occur most frequently in *Totality and Infinity*, the term desire is found in later texts as well (such as in MS, 55; OB, 88, 123, 153–62; GP, 139–40). Although terms and phrases emphasizing sacrifice, like 'substitution' and 'responsibility for the Other,' occur most frequently in *Otherwise than Being*, such terms can also be found in *Totality and Infinity* ('self-renunciation,' 253; 'exteriority,' 262; 'infinity of responsibility,' 244–45) and in *Entre Nous* ('sacrifice,' 227; 'dying for the Other,' 216; and 'responsibility for the Other,' 103, 113, 227–28). Likewise, although terms such as 'love without concupiscence' occur most frequently in *Entre Nous*, we find them as well in *Totality and Infinity* (255) and *Otherwise than Being* (123). The different emphases of these different texts is not evidence that Levinas changed his views on the subject so much as it is evidence for the complexity contained in this one consistent idea and the subtlety with which Levinas treats the topic throughout his *oeuvre*.

As further evidence of continuity of thought throughout changing terminology in Levinas's work, it can be shown that even though 'desire' occurs most frequently in TI, 'responsibility' occurs most frequently in *Otherwise than Being*, and 'love without concupiscence' occurs most frequently in *Entre Nous*, we nonetheless find all of these terms (and by extension, the other terms clustered around them) linked in significant ways. For example, in *Otherwise than Being*, Levinas says that the approach of the Other is "an assignation to a non-erotic proximity, to a desire of the non-desirable, to a desire of the stranger in the neighbor. It is outside of concupiscence," and this desire arouses an inclination "toward responsibility for the neighbor" (123). And in *Entre Nous*, love without concupiscence is linked with responsibility for the Other, such as when he speaks of the "requirement of what I call responsibility for the other, or love without concupiscence" (OUJ, 228).[34] So the passages show the strong connections between the words listed above, which help to make the case for their inclusion together as a family of terms.

While no single term can capture the essence of this family of terms, I will refer to the group of terms as 'insatiable desire' since all of these words are viewed in contrast to the terms listed in the previous section as 'satiable desire.' Levinas refers to this desire, which is insatiable desire, as 'Insatiable Desire' (TI, 63). It would seem that insatiable desire would be a term used to describe need (as Levinas uses the term), and it is often used to describe that which the ethical life must overcome,[35] but as I will explain in the following section, Levinas is using the term in a technical sense to refer to what might also be called a-satiable desire.[36] Viewing these terms together will help in understanding each of the individual terms, and likewise, looking at each of these individual terms will help in understanding the family of terms.

The 'A-satiable' in 'Insatiable Desire'

Having treated the terms associated with satiable desire in the previous section will help in the task of clarifying the way Levinas understands insatiable (a-satiable) desire. We saw there that satiable desire had three key features: 1) satiable desire comes from a state of lack, 2) satiable desire is initiated by the subject who seeks to be filled, and 3) satiable desire is capable of being satiated (the ego can live *from* the Other), even if only partially or temporarily. The a-satiability of insatiable desire can also be viewed in relation to those three features—first, it does not proceed from a privation; second, it is not initiated by the subject; and third, rather than living *from* the Other, it lives *for* the Other. I now turn to these three qualities of insatiable desire in closer detail.

Not Privation

To see this first feature of a-satiability—the fact that it is not a privation—I begin by looking at the term 'insatiable desire.' As already mentioned, this important term can be misleading if one does not understand that by insatiable desire Levinas is not referring to a desire that can never seem to get enough. Insatiable desire, in common usage, refers to a desire that is incapable of being finally satisfied, as in one's 'insatiable desire for accumulating wealth' or an 'insatiable desire for food.' The technical meaning Levinas assigns to the term is quite different, however, as is evident when he wrote, "Insatiable Desire—not because it corresponds to an infinite hunger, but because it is not an appeal for food" (TI, 63). Desire is insatiable not because of limits put on our ability to find satisfaction. It is not the fact that we will eventually want more food that causes Levinas to say that a desire is insatiable. Rather, insatiable desire is insatiable because the category of 'satiability' just does not apply to this desire. "We have just described the essential insatiability of conscience,[37] which does not belong to the order of hunger or satiety. It is thus that above we defined desire" (TI, 101).

Even though insatiable desire might normally refer to the non-satisfaction of desire, Levinas makes it quite clear that by insatiable desire he is not referring to the mere absence of satisfaction, such that might occur because there is just not enough food or not enough wealth. "This Desire is insatiable, but not because of our finitude" (TI, 63). Rather, it does not make sense to apply the description of either satiated or un-satiated, since "[d]esire does not coincide with an unsatisfied need; it is situated beyond satisfaction and non-satisfaction" (TI, 179). Another way he emphasizes the a-satiability of Desire is by describing "Desire as the 'measure' of the Infinite which no term, no satisfaction arrests" (TI, 304–5). Most directly, he denies that insatiable Desire involves satiation by writing, "in Desire there is no sinking one's teeth into being, no satiety, but an uncharted future before me" (TI, 117). So an insatiable desire, as Levinas uses the phrase, is an a-satiable desire.

The other words in this family of terms are also described as a-satiable. For example, 'metaphysics' is "an aspiration that does not proceed from a lack" (TI, 299). And the 'infinite' is defined as a-satiable: "The infinite in the finite . . . is produced as Desire—not a Desire that the possession of the Desirable slakes" (TI, 50). Using a variety of terms from this terminological group (including: infinite, metaphysics, Desire, relationship with the Other, desire of the Other, Desire for the Other, sociality, and conscience) Levinas describes a-satiable desire as that which cannot be: satiated (TI, 101), slaked (TI, 50), satisfied (MS, 51), fulfilled (TI, 179), consumed (TI, 63), possessed (TI, 50), or put to sleep (TI, 179). And again, the reason it cannot be satiated is because it is not a lack (TI, 269) or that which is lacking (MS, 51). It cannot be viewed as an unmet need (MS, 51) or viewed as that which can be arrested by satisfaction (TI, 304–5). It "does not proceed from a lack" (TI, 299), but the "metaphysical desire tends toward something else entirely, toward the absolutely other" (TI, 33–35).

Other-initiated (not Spontaneous Freedom)

A second feature of insatiable desire is that it is not self-initiated. Whereas satiable desire (need) is initiated by the subject, insatiable desire "originates from its 'object'" (TI, 62). This Other-initiated quality of insatiable desire is especially emphasized in terms such as 'passivity,' 'obsession,' and 'call.' Of these, the term 'passivity' is particularly crucial in revealing the involuntary nature of insatiable desire. Passivity does indicate that this desire is not initiated by the self, but it says more than that. Passivity, as Levinas uses the term, means more than the acceptance or reception of a thing. This passivity is not even capable of response—it is "passivity more passive still than the passivity conjoined with action" (OB, 115). It is an "absolute passivity, beneath the level of activity and passivity" (OB, 110). He is here speaking of a passivity that is not what one refers to ordinarily as passivity since even being passive can be an activity—an activity of receiving passively. What Levinas seeks to communicate by this 'absolute passivity' is that which precedes even the possibility of passive acceptance. This passivity expresses the fact that I am acted upon even before I have the opportunity to act or passively accept the action of others. The fact that I am 'for the Other' is true "prior to activity and passivity" (OB, 116). The "idea that I am sought out . . . expresses my passivity as a self" (OB, 116).

The term 'passivity' is very closely linked with Levinas's important term 'obsession.' "The most passive, unassumable, passivity . . . is due to my being obsessed with responsibility for the oppressed who is other than myself" (OB, 55). These terms are so closely linked that he speaks of both the "passivity of obsession" (OB, 55) and the "obsession of passivity" (OB, 115). And "the total passivity of obsession is more passive still than the passivity of things" (OB, 55). As we find Levinas describing obsession, the key feature, which perhaps gives it this harsh name, is the involuntary nature of this responsibility: "[W]e discern in obsession a responsibility that rests on no free commitment, a responsibility whose entry into being could be effected only without any choice" (OB, 116).

Also in this vocabulary cluster is the term 'call' which not only emphasizes the involuntary nature of insatiable desire, but also alludes to the fact that it is initiated not by some blind external cause, but by *someone*, and a someone who calls out to you in particular. The particularity of the Other-initiated call is implicit in the very word, but is even made more explicit. For example, Levinas wrote that "the beginning of language is in the face. In a certain way, in its silence, it calls *you*" (PL, 169; my emphasis). This particularity of the call or 'summons' is even more acutely described by Levinas writing that "the other in the same is my substitution for the other through respon-sibility, for which, I am summoned as someone irreplaceable" (OB, 114).

Living for the Other Rather than from the Other

Another feature of insatiable desire is that it entails a complete responsibil-ity for the Other, and this living for the Other is in contrast to living from the Other, as is true of satiable desire. This complete heteronomy is not downplayed by Levinas in his use of terminology. Rather, much of the vocabulary used to depict insatiable desire appears extremely violent. Words such as 'suffering' (TI, 238–39), 'sacrifice' (OB, 126–29), and 'substitution' (OB, 113–18) evoke images of violence and some of the terms such as 'hostage' (OB, 151), 'persecution' (OB, 166), and 'trauma' (OB, 123–25) raise the pitch even higher by emphasizing the involuntary nature of the vio-lence. These terms are not necessarily used in the ordinary sense of the words, but the charged nomenclature is most likely meant to convey the Other-initiated and absolute nature of the obligation for the Other.[38]

The 'Desire' in Insatiable Desire

It is clear, then, that Levinas is speaking of something that is a-satiable, but one might still raise the reasonable question of why he calls it a 'desire' if it has the qualities of a-satiability described above. Some might view privation as an essential feature of desire such that a-satiable desire seems to be oxy-moronic. So why does Levinas call it a desire?

Arousal of Insatiable Desire

One reason Levinas refers to insatiable desire as a desire (even though it is a-satiable) is that it involves being attracted and aroused or stirred. He describes desire as "the Desire for the Infinite which the desirable arouses rather than satisfies" (TI, 50) and "desire is an aspiration that the Desirable animates" (TI, 62). Elsewhere he similarly describes the Other as an "inspi-ration [who] arouses respiration" (OB, 116). Both satiable and insatiable desire involve an 'arousal' or an 'animation,' but in insatiable desire, this is not self-initiated. Unlike satiable desire, which arises from and is initiated by the subject, desire "originates from its 'object'" (TI, 62). Further variations of this animating terminology are seen when Levinas speaks of the "move-ment of Desire" (TI, 269) and when he "posits metaphysics as a desire," that is, a desire which is "desire engendering Desire" (TI, 304).

Although insatiable desire, as described in its violent terms, appears empty of goodness, in fact, Levinas calls this desire a "marvel" (TI, 292), a "revelation" (TI, 62), and even "goodness" (TI, 305). A persistent difference between the goodness of satiable desire and the goodness of insatiable desire is not only that the goodness of the latter is infinite, whereas the former is not; the important difference lies in the fact that this infinite goodness arises from the desired rather than from the one desiring.

Freedom of Insatiable Desire

One further question that is often raised is how something as completely heteronymous as insatiable (a-satiable) desire could be rightly called a good desire since it seems to eliminate the possibility of all autonomy. This is an important objection, and in chapters 3 and 4, I will show how this heteronomy does not annihilate autonomy. But to lay the groundwork for that, I will here list the terminology that Levinas uses to describe the freedom which this heteronomy does not destroy. He makes a distinction between genuine freedom and autonomy (OB, 118, 127, 148, 161), and most of the terms used to describe freedom can be associated with one or the other of these terms. This distinction points to a more robust view of freedom that goes beyond the 'freedom from' of autonomy toward a more genuine freedom—a 'freedom for.'[39] The terms associated with autonomy include 'spontaneity' (*spontanéité*), 'arbitrariness of the will' (*l'arbitraire du vouloir*), and 'separated being' (*l'être séparé*). These terms of autonomy are grouped with terms of satiable desire, while the terms associated with insatiable desire include 'genuine freedom' (*la liberté au sens veritable*), 'welcome' (*accueillir*), and 'here I am' (*me voici*).

Levinas does not deny the existence of autonomy, but we can see the regard he holds for it as he speaks of the "naïve arbitrariness of . . . spontaneity" (TI, 43) or of "infantile spontaneity" or "naïve spontaneity" (OB, 122) or "capricious spontaneity" (TI, 43). He also speaks of an "arbitrariness of the will" (OB, 123) and the "arbitrary dogmatism of . . . free exercise" (TI, 43). Between these two types of freedom, it is clear that this infantile, naïve, capricious, arbitrary, dogmatic autonomy does not hold pride of place, but nonetheless it does have its place.

Autonomy is also described with the term 'separated being,' and the fact that insatiable desire requires an autonomous, separated being is seen when Levinas speaks of insatiable desire as "the Desire that is the independence of the separated being and its transcendence" (TI, 269). The necessity of an autonomous, separated being is more explicitly stated when he writes,

"Revelation is discourse; in order to welcome revelation a being apt for this role of interlocutor, a separated being is required" (TI, 77).

This autonomy is also associated with the term egoism, a term which I have already shown to be linked with satiable desire. The genuine freedom of insatiable desire is both before and after the egoism of the "will's initiative"—that is, the "ego that rejoins itself in freedom" (OB, 118). The autonomy of the ego has its place but it is neither first place, nor does it have the last word, for "egoism is neither first nor last" (OB, 128). The ego, contrary to a prevalent view of philosophy, is not "the beginning or . . . the conclusion of philosophy" (OB, 127).[40]

A group of terms associated with 'genuine freedom,' however, are used to express a freedom that goes beyond autonomy. Genuine freedom is not just the addition of responsibility to balance out one's liberties, where "responsibilities correspond exactly to liberties taken, where they compensate for them." Rather, "[f]reedom in the genuine sense can be only a contestation of this book-keeping by a gratuity" (OB, 125). Genuine freedom is not something that emerges out of autonomy, but it exists before one even has the opportunity to exercise free choice. The genuine freedom of being responsible for the Other comes prior to one's acceptance or rejection of it. Before I have "a free will . . . [the Other is the] one for whom I am responsible to the point of being a hostage for him" (OB, 59).

Different from either the egoistic autonomy or the ethical genuine freedom that precedes autonomy is a type of autonomy which accepts this state of being responsible for the Other, and the term most frequently used for this convergence of genuine freedom and autonomy is 'welcome.'[41] "The Good choose[s] me first before I can be in a position to choose, that is, welcome its choice" (OB, 122). By emphasizing the precedence of genuine freedom over autonomy, he stresses that this responsibility does not emerge out of one's choice, but he nonetheless allows that I can choose to welcome or reject this responsibility.

This autonomous welcome of the preexisting responsibility is also referred to as 'hospitality' when he interchanges the terms 'desire,' 'welcome of the Other,' and 'hospitality' (TI, 254). The convergence without reduction of genuine freedom and autonomy is seen when Levinas says that hospitality is "the-one-for-the-other in the ego" (OB, 79).

Finally, the biblical phrase, 'here I am' (me voici),[42] is used in association with this convergence of freedoms; it captures both the Other-initiated quality of being called prior to one's initiation and the autonomous choice (in response) to accept that call. It implies that rather than being a 'choosing one' each individual is "a chosen one, called to leave . . . the concept of the ego to respond with responsibility: *me, that is, here I am for the others*" (OB, 185; my emphasis). The ego must leave the ego, but must be an ego in order to be able to choose to leave it. This 'here I am' "signifies me in the name of God, at the service of men that look at me, without having anything to identify myself with, but the sound of my voice" (OB, 149). This response is thus not an assertion of the ego's identity, but an acceptance of one's identity as residing in the very call of the Other.

To summarize this distinction between 'need' (satiable desire) and 'desire' (insatiable desire), I turn to a later essay written between the completion of *Totality and Infinity* and *Otherwise than Being* in which Levinas wrote, "such is [insatiable] desire: to burn with another fire than need, which saturation extinguishes, to think beyond what one thinks. Because of this inassimilable surplus, because of this *beyond*, we have called the relationship which links the I with the Other the idea of the Infinite" (MS, 55). Here we see that this is a desire because it is a burning, but it is a-satiable because it cannot be self-initiated (as if in isolation) but must rely on the Other, who is beyond the category of satisfaction or nonsatisfaction. He goes on to say, "The idea of the infinite is Desire. It paradoxically consists in thinking more than what is thought and maintaining what is thought in this very excess relative to thought—in entering into a relationship with the ungraspable while guaranteeing its status of being ungraspable" (MS, 55). This speaks of both the positive and negative descriptions of a-satiable desire—the fact that one is able to be in relationship with the infinite is the positive description of desire, and it explains why it is appropriate to call this a desire. Yet, he also speaks of it as ungraspable, which is to describe it negatively: as that which cannot be devoured as if I had a hunger for it, which a grasping might somehow satisfy.

Chapter 3

Levinasian Love

La philosophie: sagesse de *l'amour* au service de *l'amour*

Levinas writes, "Philosophy is the wisdom of love in the service of love" (OB, 162), which he juxtaposes with the traditional philosophical love of wisdom. En route to answering the question of how this wisdom of love differs from the love of wisdom, this chapter will focus on what Levinas meant by 'love.'

The single term 'love,' as explained in chapter 2, includes two subsets of terms, which I grouped around 'need' (or 'satiable desire') and 'desire' (or 'a-satiable desire' as defined in chapter 2). In chapter 2, I showed the interrelation of terms grouped with need or satiable desire that include '*eros*,' 'hunger,' 'void,' the 'for-itself,' 'egoism,' 'separation,' 'interiority,' 'concupiscence,' 'satiation,' 'enjoyment,' 'sensibility,' 'consumption,' 'satisfaction,' 'possession,' and 'living from.'

As we also saw in chapter 2, the subset of interrelated Levinasian terms grouped with desire or insatiable desire include 'metaphysical desire,' 'exteriority,' 'love without concupiscence,' 'love without *eros*,' 'love of one's neighbor,' '*agape*,' 'ethical relation,' 'conscience,' 'infinity,' 'authority,' 'saying,' 'disinterestedness,' 'responsibility,' 'revelation,' 'holiness,' 'call,' 'accusation,' 'substitution,' 'incarnation,' 'suffering,' 'sacrifice,' 'hostage,' 'persecution,' 'obsession,' 'trauma,' 'host,' 'welcome,' 'genuine freedom,' 'independence,' 'attraction,' 'aspiration,' 'marvel,' 'goodness,' 'care,' and 'grace.' In chapter 2, we saw some of the key distinguishing factors between these two types of love or desire. The goal of this chapter is to examine how Levinas saw these two types of love *relating* to each other, and I will do so by addressing a series of

43

questions that have wide-ranging answers in the secondary literature. I will sort through that literature and not only argue for a particular interpretation, but I will offer explanations for the interpretive variance when appropriate.

First, I will ask whether Levinas saw need and desire as completely distinct or whether he thought one type of love could be reduced and explained in terms of the other type of love.[1] In other words, is it possible to reduce 'neighbor-love'[2] (a-satiable, sacrificial, *agape*, altruistic love) to 'concupiscence' (satiable, possessing, hungry, consumptive love) or vice versa? Or are they both irreducible to the other type of love? Then I will ask whether Levinas thought that occurrences of pure neighbor-love were empirically possible. Replies to that question will raise the further question of whether or not Levinas's position on these matters is a coherent one or whether he was simply describing an impossible ideal to pursue. If we take his talk of asymmetry as describing a coherent possibility, rather than a flat contradiction or a mere hyperbole, then we must face the question of how that is so.

Some of the views we will examine seek to preserve the possibility and asymmetry of his view at the cost of embracing reductionism. Others will seek to hold on to Levinas's asymmetry and nonreductionism by giving up on the possibility of such a neighbor-love actually occurring. Other interpretations have Levinas holding a nonreductionist neighbor-love that is possible, but do so by understating or misstating the asymmetry. I contend that Levinas holds a view of neighbor-love such that it is empirically possible, it is not reducible to concupiscence, and it remains asymmetrical in important ways. Critics might accuse me of letting Levinas have his cake, give it away, and eat it too, but we shall see by taking it one piece at a time.

§1 Was Levinas a Reductionist?

The first view I will examine is that of reductionism with regard to neighbor-love and concupiscence. Although there is wide agreement in the secondary literature that Levinas was clearly not offering a reductionist view of neighbor-love and concupiscence that would understand neighbor-love merely as a derivative form of concupiscence, the unusual alternative of reductionism (of all concupiscence being a form of neighbor-love) does have an advocate. Jeffrey Bloechl interprets Levinas as a reductionist, but not as the usual sort of reductionist, such as Sartre, for example, who says that neighbor-love (or *agape*) is "in fact no more than an especially complex form of self-interest." Bloechl argues that neighbor-love, which is "my attachment to you, [is] not merely in spite of your otherness but first because of it."[3] Erotic or concupiscent love, as Bloechl interprets Levinas, presupposes neighbor-love, is experienced through neighbor-love, and is therefore a form of neighbor-love. Even if you allow that concupiscence presupposes neighbor-love and that concupiscence is experienced through neighbor-love, it does not follow that it is a form of neighbor-love. He tries to convince us of the reduction of concupiscence to neighbor-love by saying that "Levinas's own analysis of the rise and fall of erotic desire teaches nothing if not this: at the end of my desire, and thus also throughout it, this other person remains other."[4] That the Other is Other, even when I have only erotic regard for her, implies that her otherness is not dependent on my recognizing it. That seems to me quite accurate, but it does not give us a reduction of concupiscence to neighbor-love. The coexistence of two things does not entail their conflation. Bloechl may raise some interesting points about the relationship between concupiscence and neighbor-love, but he provides no convincing argument for the reduction of concupiscence to neighbor-love.

Furthermore, Levinas quite explicitly avoids reductionism of both kinds. In case it was not already obvious, he clearly rejects the reduction of neighbor-love to concupiscence, such as we might find in Freud.[5] But he also rejects the reduction of concupiscence to neighbor-love. That neighbor-love (*agape*) and concupiscence (*eros*) are distinct is hinted at by some of the ways he describes neighbor-love. For example, he often refers to neighbor-love as "love without *Eros*" or "love without concupiscence" (NC, 131). And finally, the most obvious rejection of reductionism is seen when he flatly rejects such a reduction, saying, "I don't think that *Agape* comes from *Eros*," and, "*Eros* is definitely not *Agape*" (PJL, 113).

Acknowledging the consensus[6] opinion in the secondary literature that Levinas viewed neighbor-love and concupiscence as distinct and irreducible to each other, we can now turn to the next question of whether occurrences of a nonreductionist neighbor-love are empirically possible.

§2 Is Neighbor-Love Impossible?

If one takes a nonreductionist view of neighbor-love, as Levinas does, the reply by some is that such a view can only be held hypothetically or hyperbolically. Since it is the view of some that neighbor-love never appears without the presence of concupiscence, thinking that neighbor-love and concupiscence are separable can only be an impossible ideal toward which one strives. This is how Derrida, and many others reading Levinas through Derridean spectacles, viewed Levinas's nonreductionist neighbor-love.

Derrida thinks it is noble to pursue such an ideal, but we must not fool ourselves by thinking that the ideal can be actualized.

Derrida

Much of the recent work by Derrida and others on the topic of the impossibility of neighbor-love has revolved around the discussion of "the Gift."[7] Derrida discusses at length the impossibility of a pure gift in *Given Time*. There he says that we speak of pure giving, but nowhere see it actually occurring. He writes that "the word 'gift' is always cited, mentioned, but nowhere used. The complication does not depend only on a word concerning which it is unclear under what conditions, finally one could ever rightfully use it. *The Gift* complicates itself, *gets taken up* [*se prend*] in its own internal complication: giving itself to be an essay on the gift, it is also in truth an essay on taking."[8] He is saying that with any act of giving, there is also an act of taking, which nullifies the gift as such. There is always give and take, he says, and with the persistent presence of reciprocity there can be no pure neighbor-love when neighbor-love is taken to be the absence of taking.

Derrida's source for this treatment of the gift is our common language and understanding of giving. He says that he is just making explicit what he knows and what we know 'gift' and 'to give' "mean in our common language and logic." Drawing from his "precomprehension of what *gift* means," he makes two key points—one regarding the structure of the gift and the other regarding the necessary condition of a gift. The structure of the gift is such that someone "(A) intends-to-give B to C" or in other words "if giving indeed means what, in speaking of it among ourselves, we think it means, then it is necessary, in a certain situation, that some 'one' give some 'thing' to some 'one other.'" Also drawing on our common understanding, he says that "for there to be a gift there must be no reciprocity, return, exchange, countergift, or debt."[9] If this is the necessary structure and condition for a gift to be given, then it raises the following problem.

If a gift is presented to the recipient, as the structure requires, then there is always something received in return—either by way of an actual gift given in exchange, or even by some word of thanks. Even if the gift is given anonymously, the donor still receives a sense of satisfaction for having given. Reciprocity can even occur at the conscious or unconscious level.

Reciprocity, so understood, always occurs when someone gives something to someone. And this leads to the *aporia:* "These conditions of possibility of the gift . . . designate simultaneously the conditions of the impossibility of the gift." Therefore, "these conditions of possibility define or produce the annulment, the annihilation, the destruction of the gift."[10] In brief, that is how Derrida carries out his deconstruction of the possibility of neighbor-love, so defined.

Caputo

John Caputo is convinced by Derrida's deconstruction of absolute altruism[11] and therefore takes neighbor-love to be impossible since even the most anonymous, selfless, unaware act of sacrifice is finally infected with some degree of self-interest. As Caputo puts it, "I do want to be absolutely altruistic . . . I want to. But if that is what I want, then if I am altruistic I end up doing what I want."[12] And no matter how negligible the emphasis upon the "I want" may be, he shows that we can never shake the "I want" or the "for me."

Caputo, following the example of Derrida, suggests that impossibility is not something to dread, but to love. The impossible is not something to be pursued despite its impossibility but because of it. To the contrary, he endorses the claim by Johannes Climacus that "the lover of the merely possible is a mediocre fellow."[13] But when Levinas tells us about the absolute altruistic obligation for the Other, we do not find him saying that this is merely an impossible ideal towards which we should strive. To the contrary, according to Levinas, our obligation to be wholly for the other is presented as an empirical fact. It is in the midst of this discussion of the undeconstructed Levinas that Caputo says, "Levinas—if you insist on taking him straight, without a twist of deconstruction—is too pious, [and] his poetics are too grave."[14]

While retaining respect for Levinas and his absolute altruistic obligation to the Other, Caputo nonetheless concludes that it is absolutely impossible to fulfill this demand. Caputo writes that the "'absolutely Other' of which Levinas speaks is a fabulous story. I am speaking sincerely, literally. The 'absolutely Other' is a gripping tale, very moving and very powerful, a tremendous and salutary shock that Levinas delivers to contemporary philosophy." But the emphasis is upon the fiction—the poetry—the fabulous nature of this story of obligation. Caputo thinks that Levinas goes to excess and uses "a bit of hyperbole." The altruism or neighbor-love of which Levinas speaks is "an impossible dream."[15]

There are two common responses to Levinas on this point by those who, like Derrida and Caputo, see this altruism as empirically impossible. One response is to take Levinas as speaking literally, reject his view on the subject as incoherent, and dismiss it for creating a false understanding of ourselves.

Another response is to say that he is speaking hyperbolically in an attempt to get us closer to this impossible ideal, and to therefore embrace the view as ethically edifying. Derrida and Caputo generally take him to be speaking literally, but try to nudge him into admitting that what he is really doing is speaking in hyperbole.

First I will look at two other examples of those who see Levinas's love for the Other as an impossibility but think that Levinas is exaggerating with a noble purpose. Then I will turn to two others who think that the impossibility is grounds for dismissal.

Sublime Impossibility

Stephen Webb tries to come to Levinas's defense by suggesting that the critics who accuse him of presenting the impossible as possible, are taking him too literally. Webb says that what "these criticisms of Levinas miss is that his rhetoric as well as his method is hyperbolic precisely because he cannot philosophize as usual about the fundamental situation of being obligated." Webb describes Levinas's language of absolute obligation to the Other as a "continuous mode of exaggeration, acceleration, and intensification. Indeed, hyperbole, due to its alleged irrationality, is the perfect trope for a project that tries to say what cannot be said."[16] But for all that "irrationality," Webb endorses such language of excess and hyperbole for how it might motivate one to act.

Richard Kearney, as well, speaks of the impossibility of the gift. In his treatment of 'the problem of the gift,' Kearney says that he is trying to "take [the gift] out of the circle of economy, of exchange, but *not* to conclude, from the impossibility for the gift to appear as such and to be determined as such, to its absolute impossibility."[17]

In another essay in the same volume, Kearney connects Levinas's hyperbolic style with the impossibility of his ethic, suggesting that the exaggeration is a sign of the impossibility of that which Levinas speaks. "For the very hyperbolic excess of Levinas's ethics is, arguably, the very token of its impossibility." Kearney ends his treatment of Levinas in this essay by quoting Caputo and joining in his awe of the sublimity of Levinas's excess—even if it is scandalously impossible.[18]

Problematic Impossibility

Not all who find Levinas's neighbor-love impossible remain so friendly toward it. Robyn Horner, for example, finds Levinas's neighbor-love impossible, and instead of delighting in that impossibility, as Derrida, Caputo, and Kearney seem to, she faults him for it. Levinas's "absolute asymmetry is problematic," she claims, "because it leaves no prospect for my own alterity for the Other." If it is impossible, as she thinks it is, then it has the problem in application to life as we live it, since life as we live it always contains some type of reciprocity. Unlike those mentioned earlier who think that this impossibility is sublime in some sense, Horner does not find it helpful because it does not accurately describe life as we find it. And if it is not an accurate description of ourselves and the way we love, then it ceases to be of any use as an ethical guide. The impossibility of this neighbor-love "breaks down the possibility of any general application of Levinas's thinking." In life, there is always reciprocity, but with Levinas, as she interprets him, there "can be no reciprocity." This "does not sit well in the human context."[19]

Also interpreting Levinas as embracing an impossible ethic, but much more severe in his criticism of it is Paul Ricoeur. Ricoeur also accuses Levinas's description of the neighbor-love as excessive, but to Ricoeur, this is not some virtuous use of hyperbole, but is a most vicious and irresponsible use—that is, abuse—of language that has no redeeming qualities to it. Ricoeur lists one hyperbole after another pointing to Levinas's notion of subject as 'hostage' as "the most excessive of all." His disapproval of this hyperbole is quite clear. "By hyperbole, it must be strongly underscored, we are not to understand a figure of style, a literary trope, but the systematic practice of excess in philosophical argumentation."[20]

Ricoeur thinks Levinas should give up on this impossible philosophy, not only because he thinks it is impossible but because he thinks it is an inaccurate account of the self. What then should be done with the philosophy of Levinas? Does Levinas's philosophy claim that the impossible is possible? Does he thereby commit himself to an incoherent view, as Derrida and the others accuse him if he is to be taken literally? If that is the case (although I am not saying it is), then could his philosophy be salvaged, repaired, and modified by taking Ricoeur's advice? If we modified Levinas's philosophy by introducing the type of reciprocity Ricoeur advocates—that is, a reciprocal relationship that is fundamentally based on self-esteem and interacts with the Other on an Aristotelian[21] model of friendship of *philia*—mutual giving and receiving—would we thereby make Levinas coherent?[22] If we 'Ricoeured' Levinas, would we thereby cure him of his alleged excessive philosophical inconsistencies?

To the contrary, one could make a strong argument that so modifying Levinas's views would not cure them of contradiction but in fact make him undeniably incoherent. To make reciprocity fundamental, and to make the self the initiator of ethical obligation, as Ricoeur does, would be to overturn Levinas's central point—his point that the ethical relation is initiated by the Other and not the self. Even Ricoeur notices this significant difference and writes, "E. Levinas's entire philosophy rests on the initiative of the other in the intersubjective relation. In reality, this initiative establishes no relation at all, to the extent that the other represents absolute exteriority with respect to an ego defined by the condition of separation. The other, in this sense, absolves himself of any relation. This irrelation defines exteriority as such."[23]

Although I do not have space here to give a full response to Ricoeur, I defer to Richard Cohen's response to Ricoeur. Besides pointing out, correctly, in my view, that Ricoeur misrepresents and therefore misunderstands this view of the Other, Cohen shows us that the "differences separating Ricoeur and Levinas are sharp." One of these sharp differences is that "Ricoeur's hierarchy of the self and other is exactly the reverse of Levinas's, for whom moral sociality precedes moral character."[24] So it seems clear enough that not only does Levinas think quite differently than Ricoeur on the hierarchy of the self in the ethical relationship to the Other, but to add this sort of basic mutuality into Levinas's philosophy would not rescue it from alleged contradiction, but would make it contradictory at the core.

Irigaray

Another criticism of Levinas's view of *eros* comes from Luce Irigaray, and hers strikes a severe blow if her reading is correct. As she reads Levinas's relation between ethical love and erotic love in "Phenomenology of Eros" in *Totality and Infinity*, Irigaray sees *eros* as that through which the male passes in order to reach the transcendence of the ethical. The female beloved embodies *eros*, while the male lover moves through and beyond this *eros* in order to achieve ethical love. Irigaray writes that "[b]etween blind nostalgia and ethical tension, the male lover loves and despises himself through the beloved woman. . . . He attracts and rejects himself through this other, while he takes on neither infancy nor animality."[25] The problem is that this move to the ethical and the divine is not accessible within the female experience, according to her interpretation. This protest is most explicit in "Questions to Emmanuel Levinas."[26] "This description of pleasure given by Levinas is unacceptable to the extent that it presents man as the sole subject exercising his desire and his appetite upon the woman who is deprived of subjectivity except to seduce him."[27] This critique strongly suggests that the two loves are incompatible.

Following Irigaray, Tina Chanter underscores the difference between the two loves by contrasting the role of reciprocity in each. A "difference between the relation of *eros* and that of the face to face, is that in the latter relation there is no return to self." The differentiating factor is reciprocity, and this actual presence of any reciprocity is enough to cause ethical love to vanish. The incompatibility of reciprocity and ethical love is clear for Irigaray and Chanter. "Of course, there is a reciprocity" but "once the asymmetry disappears . . . 'I and other become interchangeable in commerce'" (TI, 226).[28] Reciprocity, even unintended, spoils the ethical love.

The brunt of Irigaray's critique comes when that incompatibility of *eros* and ethics is combined with a view that equates the feminine with the erotic. Chanter summarizes Irigaray's critique (which seems to be her critique as well) saying that "the description of pleasure given by Levinas is unacceptable to the extent that it presents man as the sole subject exercising his desire and his appetite upon the woman who is deprived of subjectivity except to seduce him."[29] So the ethical, while distinct from the erotic, is exclusively available to the male.

Stella Sandford also follows Irigaray's criticism of Levinas, but takes a slightly different view of the relationship between ethical love and *eros*. Rather than seeing the two loves as incompatible, she speaks of their coexistence. "In love both desire and need, metaphysical desire and erotic desire, transcendence and concupiscence, coexist." And their coexistence is not merely by way of taking turns, but the compatibility is one that can occur simultaneously. Sandford writes that it "is not that 'now one, now another' exists, but that both prevail and that this ambiguity and simultaneity is the very essence of love."[30]

Even though Sandford views these two loves as compatible, she finally rejects Levinas's view of *eros* since she sees it as undermining her feminist project. Her reason for making this claim comes for different reasons than Irigaray, however. It is not that worldly erotic love and the transcendent ethical love are separate and the feminine is earth-bound in *eros*. *Eros* and ethical love reside together, contends Sandford, but Levinas's fault lies in allowing them to reside in transcendence. Even though she finds much in Levinas with which she is sympathetic, she nonetheless summarizes her rejection of his view as follows:

> From an external viewpoint, however, and one which would point frankly to the strong stream of Judaic patriarchalism bearing Levinas's philosophical reflection along, the more basic point is that the future of a twenty-first century feminist politics never was going to be found in a metaphysics of transcendence. Such a metaphysics remains fundamentally incompatible

with a feminist theoretical project which aims to help transform society
through the location of the origin of meanings . . . in the finite structures
of the world.[31]

Sandford ultimately finds Levinas androcentric not because he excludes the
feminine from the transcendent, but because he allows for transcendence at all.
This compatibility of *eros* and ethical love comes at the expense of transcendence. Is reduction of the two loves the only way for them to be compatible?

In a most careful and nuanced reading of Levinas on *eros*, Claire Katz
avoids the usual dichotomy between reductionistic compatibilism and nonreductionistic incompatibilism. Katz agrees with the crucial point of Irigaray,
that we must not abandon sexual difference in the account of sexuality.

"Irigaray is correct, in my view, to claim that the Other cannot be
thought of without thinking it in terms of sexual difference" but is "mistaken
when she assumes the Beloved is always the woman."[32] Just as in the Song
of Songs, sometimes the male is the beloved, and sometimes the female is the
lover.

While siding with Irigaray on the importance of sexual difference, Katz
parts from Irigaray in that Katz does not find Levinas detaching the ethical
from the erotic. Katz writes that "[t]his point, the relationship between the
erotic and the ethical, is worth dwelling on for a moment, since this is precisely the issue for Irigaray—the erotic relation is not ethical." Katz, however,
sees that "[f]or Levinas, this relationship is more complex than that for
which Irigaray has accounted. For Levinas, the erotic conceals the ethical."
This does not mean that the erotic is mutually exclusive with the ethical, but
that the ethical can be present in the erotic. Perhaps, Katz suggests, Levinas's
view of the erotic is not as simple or as easily dismissed as some of his critics think. Perhaps, she posits, Levinas has "described the erotic more accurately than we think." This subtle view is hinted at by saying that "the ethical
hides behind the erotic. The ethical is not absent."[33]

Katz does not exclude the ethical from the erotic, but neither does Katz
reduce one of the loves to the other, as Sandford and others have done. Even
while she sees that Levinas does not exclude the ethical from the erotic, Katz
nonetheless sees them as irreducibly distinct. "This love [eros] is not to be
confused with the Christian *agape*!" "Love in the 'Phenomenology of Eros'
is not the purified love of Beatrice."[34]

The Gift 'As Such'

Katz[35] hints that there may be a way to understand Levinas's ethical love for
the Other compatible with *eros* without being reduced to the erotic. Some

may wonder if this can be done without saying that the ethical neighbor-love is either impossible or incoherent. A brief comment by Kearney gives us a clue as to why that is not the only option. Kearney is among the interpreters I described earlier who agree with Derrida's deconstruction of the altruistic gift in general and Levinas's altruistic neighbor-love, in particular. But Kearney made an important qualification when he said that the gift was impossible. As cited earlier, he said that the "gift as such is impossible. I insist on the 'as such.' "[36] Why does he make such a fuss about the 'as such'? That 'as such' is referring to the gift as described by Derrida—namely that there be an absolute absence of reciprocity. Derrida may have successfully deconstructed the gift as such, but that raises the question of whether this is an accurate description of altruism, and whether this was the description of altruistic neighbor-love that Levinas embraced.

To trace this view of the gift quickly as such, we can find that most of the interpreters I cited above have referred in some way or other to Derrida's description of the gift. Derrida himself said he was just drawing upon a common understanding of the gift—a 'precomprehension' found in common language describing what we all know to be true about giving and gifts.[37] But, if that is the case, how complete and how accurate is this description?[38] If this is just a 'common understanding' of giving, how does he explain the many people who do not agree that giving requires an absolute absence of reciprocity? For example, John Milbank suggests that some types of reciprocity certainly do annul a gift. But he describes his own precomprehension of the gift to allow for some types of reciprocity when a reciprocated gift is given after a delay of time and if it differs sufficiently from the gift received.[39] So, it is not clear that our common understanding supports such a view of the gift. One may even wonder how much influence Nietzsche's view of neighbor-love[40] had on Derrida's precomprehension.

But whether or not Derrida and the others accurately analyze the gift as impossible, I want to ask whether Levinas held this view. Derrida's analysis of giving seems to me to be much narrower than that of Levinas. Derrida seems entirely focused on the giving and the getting. Vicious reciprocity has occurred if there is any *thing* that is given back or received back, and this is ignoring the fact that other variables, such as the motives or intentions of the giver, might have bearing on the quality of the gift. One might agree, for example, that neighbor-love remains pure neighbor-love even in the case where something is returned to the donor, just so long as the motive for giving was not the *expectation* of return. There are, of course, many voices in the theological discussion of neighbor-love (*agape*)[41] which allow that actual return to the self does not necessarily negate the quality of the giving. That group of views I will refer to by the name compatibilism, since such views hold that neighbor-love is compatible with concupiscence. If Levinas held a compatibilist view of neighbor-love and concupiscence, then we may see that his claim of asymmetrical love of the other is not merely a pipe dream or a foolish incongruity, but something that demands action and something that is possible.

§3 Was Levinas a Compatibilist?

Even though Derrida's gift 'as such' may be impossible, might Levinas have held a view that did not describe giving as Derrida did? I want to ask whether Levinas in fact held a compatibilist view of neighbor-love and concupiscence. A related question is whether Levinas *could* have held such a position without it contradicting his ideas in some crucial way.[42]

Levinas as Compatibilist

One of the strongest advocates for the interpretation that Levinas was indeed a compatibilist is Adriaan Peperzak. Peperzak does not find Levinas saying that the transcendence of neighbor-love must necessarily preclude any trace of the immanence of concupiscence. As Peperzak explains it, neither the this-worldliness of concupiscence nor the other-worldliness of neighbor-love makes the other impossible. Rather, "turning to the otherwise and the height of the 'elsewhere' is not . . . fleeing away from worldliness." And likewise, "[l]oyalty to the human world does not imply at all the betrayal of all transcendence."[43]

Recalling that for Levinas 'desire' (*desir*) is the term associated with neighbor-love, and 'need' (*besoin*) is the term associated with concupiscence, we can see that Peperzak clearly views Levinas as a compatibilist when he says that this "desire of 'a future never future enough,' [is] in contrast to, *and* in union with, the needy and consumptive part of love."[44] But is it possible for neighbor-love to be both in contrast to and in union with concupiscence?

"The relation between the Same (or the totality) and the Other . . . characterizes the Other as a reality that cannot be integrated or 'sublated' into any consciousness, spirit, or other form of interiority." The Other, which requires neighbor-love, and the Same, which is full of concupiscence, cannot be integrated in this totalizing way. Neighbor-love (desire) and concupiscence (need) remain irreducible, reminding us that "Desire . . . must be sharply distinguished from any form of need."[45] But still they both can be present within a person—they can remain distinct while coexisting simultaneously within the agent.

The way that these can be nondestructively joined together is, perhaps, best explained when Peperzak writes that "transcendence does not condemn the joys of life, but it prevents them from becoming absolute; it despises idolatry." Peperzak suggests that Levinas, even if strongly asymmetrical, does not necessarily rule out the option of what Peperzak calls "double asymmetry," and he emphasizes that Levinas says, "I myself can feel myself to be the other of the other" (OB, 84). Peperzak takes this to mean "the asymmetry of this relation does not seem to exclude a double asymmetry in which I am as 'high' for the Other as the Other is for me."[46] So compatibilists, like Peperzak, view neighbor-love and concupiscence as existing together even though they cannot be reduced to either concupiscence or neighbor-love. The point is that neighbor-love can flourish despite the co-presence of concupiscence.

Merold Westphal also interprets Levinas as a compatibilist, but makes a more sober judgment than Peperzak about the ease with which this can occur. Within the bounds of Levinas's thought, he acknowledges that neighbor-love is possible, but nonetheless remains very difficult. Why is that? First, Westphal makes it clear that the commanded neighbor-love is in contrast to self-love. "As both Levinas and Kierkegaard emphasize, neighbor love runs counter to our natural self love," and as such, taken seriously, "the command to practice it is truly traumatic. How at all, is it possible, even imperfectly?"[47] Even while admitting the apparent impossibility, he adds that such a commanded love is made possible by being loved—this allows one to subordinate self-love to neighbor-love.

However, while Kierkegaard does offer us hope of this love received, Levinas, Westphal explains, does not. And since Levinas's talk of God as absolutely transcendent makes God distant to the "point of absence," Levinas does not seem to offer much hope of being loved by such a God. If we cannot be loved by God, but are still given the command to love the neighbor, this is possibly "a recipe for despair and even cynicism." In the end, however, Westphal finds that Levinas does not absolutely deny God's presence or love, and that this, while not overly hopeful, is nonetheless not hopeless—it serves rather to underscore the extreme difficulty[48] (though not impossibility) of acting out this love of the neighbor.

Easy or difficult, the view is that concupiscence undermines neighbor-love, and that the command requires "the subordination of self-love to neighbor love."[49] And this view is supported by Levinas when he writes that "love of one's neighbor . . . [is] love in which the ethical aspect dominates the passionate aspect" (PJL, 103).

Levinas Could Have Been a Compatibilist

There are other interpreters of Levinas who do not go so far as to say that Levinas *was* a compatibilist, but insist that he *could* have been a compatibilist. Olthuis and John Davenport, for example, view Levinas this way.[50] When Olthuis and Davenport make sense of Levinas's asymmetrical understanding of neighbor-love, they are not convinced that this was a necessary move on Levinas's part. They contend that neighbor-love and concupiscence can be viewed as mutually supporting. Rather than concupiscence being the parasite on neighbor-love, both Davenport and Olthuis suggest a sort of symbiotic relationship between the two types of love.

Davenport, for example, takes Levinas to be embracing an absolute asymmetry with regard to neighbor-love (*agape*) and concupiscence (*eros*), interpreting Levinas as not "allowing any reciprocity into originary *agape*." He characterizes Levinas's 'metaphysical desire' as a view of neighbor-love that could be seen as what Gene Outka describes as a "self-renunciatory" conception of *agape*, as opposed to a "reconciliation" conception of *agape*.[51] By saying that Levinas's *agape* is of the "self-renunciatory" type, he means that Levinas's understanding of *agape* completely lacks any allowance for reciprocity, whereas "reconciliation" views allow for some type or degree of reciprocity.

Olthuis also takes Levinas to be advocating an absolute asymmetry. He writes about Levinas's ethical relation saying that his "implication is that an activity is not ethical unless there is a complete lack of self-interest and self-concern" since "such concern for self is, in his view, the non-ethical ontological self inevitably closed in on its own self-interest. Disinterest, expiation, total subjection to the other regardless of his/her motivations is what it means to be ethical."[52]

Olthuis, though, views Levinas's asymmetry as an attempt to preserve neighbor-love from being reduced to concupiscence, but thinks that neighbor-love can be preserved otherwise. Olthuis raises the question of "whether in (rightly) challenging narcissistic self-interest, Levinas doesn't (inadvisedly) bring into ethical disrepute all concern for self-interest." Pure neighbor-love requires the absence of selfishness, but he thinks, "Genuine mutuality includes a self-love which is not . . . selfishness." In a comment indicating Olthuis's understanding of neighbor-love and concupiscence as potentially symbiotic, he writes: "In the interstices of love, Nygren's antithesis of *eros* and *agape* notwithstanding, mutuality can be a sojourn together in which loving self and loving other need not be in opposition but may be mutually enriching."[53]

Both Davenport and Olthuis think that Levinas is not a compatibilist, but that he *could* be if he simply admitted that neighbor-love and concupiscence can potentially coexist in a mutually supportive way. This is an interesting point, and one that is helpful for the discussion. I think we can agree with Davenport and Olthuis that Levinas could be a compatibilist;[54] I think it is worth discovering whether he really was or not.

A 'Third' Look at Compatibilism

Before I turn to some conclusions about Levinas's views on these matters, I should make note of one important qualification: it is generally agreed that if Levinas was a compatibilist, it was only when 'the third'[55] was present. For example, even one of the strongest representatives of the compatibilist interpretation—Peperzak—admits that compatibilism is only an option after the arrival of the third. Peperzak makes the important qualification that "Levinas insists on the non-reciprocity of the relationship between the Other and me [before the third arrives]."[56] The compatibilism of 'double asymmetry' only enters into the relation when the third is introduced. At the primordial level (before the third is introduced), "neither reciprocity nor dialogical relations are possible."[57]

This is made clear by Levinas who writes that "with the third party . . . I now pass from the relation without reciprocity to a relation in which there is reciprocity" (PO, 102). Since most of those who interpret Levinas as a compatibilist recognize that this only applies under the condition of the presence of the third, I will focus on the situation where the third has already arrived. That said, I now turn to my conclusions regarding Levinas's understanding of the relationship of neighbor-love and concupiscence.

§4 Does Asymmetry Preach?

After considering these many possible interpretations of Levinas's neighbor-love, can we conclude whether or not he was a compatibilist? And if he was a compatibilist, then what sort of compatibilist was he, and how, if at all, is that consistent with all of his talk about asymmetry?

Asymmetrical Prolegomena

At least as early as *Totality and Infinity*, we can see that Levinas is probably compatibilist when he speaks of the "simultaneity of need and desire" (255) in a section called "The Ambiguity of Love" (254–55). But the fact that reciprocity (as things received in return for giving) does not necessarily negate neighbor-love can be seen more clearly in many of his later essays. For example, when he says that love-without-concupiscence (neighbor-love) "is originally without reciprocity" (OUJ, 228), we see an even stronger clue that the salient factor in determining neighbor-love is not on the thing returned. It is only *originally* without reciprocity, which leaves open the possibility of neighbor-love remaining neighbor-love even if it is not *finally* without reciprocity.

It becomes quite unambiguous, however, by the time he wrote the essay "Useless Suffering" that Levinas held that reciprocity does not necessarily annul neighbor-love. He writes that "[t]he interhuman . . . is prior to any contract that would specify precisely the moment of reciprocity—a point at which altruism and disinterestedness may, to be sure, continue, but at which they may also diminish or die out" (US, 100). This single passage reveals much about agapeistic altruism. First, we see that, unlike many of the discussions I have been examining in this chapter, Levinas focuses not on the gift given or received, but on the *interhuman* desire.[58] Secondly, we also see that unlike many of the discussions reviewed so far, Levinas's emphasis is not on the initiative of the giver but on the initiative of the Other. The interhuman *is prior to any contract*, so this occurs before I have the opportunity to voluntarily choose my responsibilities. Thirdly, and importantly, we see in the quote above that even when reciprocity is introduced into pure altruism, that altruism *may, to be sure, continue*. It cannot be said much more clearly than that. It is possible that altruism continue to be altruism even after there is reciprocity. If we can admit, then, that Levinas was a compatibilist, the question that arises is this: what sort of compatibilism does he embrace?

Asymmetrical Motives

As I hinted earlier, Levinas's asymmetry goes beyond the single variable of reciprocity of *thingness*. He is not concerned just with whether some *thing* is given back or received by the donor. What then makes an action agapeistic or altruistic?

A deciding factor in asymmetry for Levinas has to be the donor's motive. When Levinas was asked, "But is not the Other also responsible in my regard?" Levinas's answer was very revealing. He said, "Perhaps, but that is *his* affair. One of the fundamental themes of *Totality and Infinity* . . . is that the intersubjective relation is a non-symmetrical relation. In this sense, I am responsible for the Other without waiting for reciprocity, were I to die for it" (EI, 98; emphasis in original). So we see quite clearly that he does not rule out the possibility that the Other might be responsible for me in the way I am responsible for the Other. If he thought that the Other being for me would negate my asymmetrical love for the Other, then he would simply have answered the above question with a "no" rather than a "perhaps." After giving the answer above, he restates the underlining fact that asymmetry requires that I not seek reciprocity. Levinas says, "Reciprocity is *his* affair" (EI, 98; emphasis in original). What is crucial here for Levinas's asymmetry is that I am not concerning myself with whether or not the Other will reciprocate.

Perhaps the poor young couple in O. Henry's "The Gift of the Magi" demonstrates this principle of asymmetry in that each of them gives to the Other without concerning themselves with whether the Other will reciprocate. She sacrifices her most treasured possession (her hair) to buy him a chain for her husband's most prized possession (his watch). But simultaneously, he sells his watch to buy her some expensive combs for her hair. Each of them makes a sacrifice for the sake of the other, but each of them also is the beneficiary of the other's sacrificial, asymmetrical giving.[59] If this is analyzed on a narrow thing-based understanding of the gift, a la Derrida, we would have to say that no gifts were given. Levinas, however, would not say that the gift was annulled by receiving something in return.

Further underscoring this emphasis upon motive, Levinas concludes an important essay by explaining that it "is in the interhuman perspective of my responsibility for the other, without concern for reciprocity, in my call for his or her disinterested help, in the asymmetry of the relation of *one* to the *other*, that I have tried to analyze the phenomenon of useless suffering" (US, 101; my emphasis). Here again, we have the reminder of the *inter*human quality of this asymmetrical relation, and that the reason it is asymmetrical is that in my responsibility for the Other, I act *without concern for* reciprocity.

Asymmetrical Conscience

The objection will immediately be raised as to how this emphasis upon motive and intention affects his view of ethical action. Is altruism for Levinas merely a matter, then, of having good intentions? In short, no. While my motive may be of great importance, good intention is not a sufficient condition for altruism.

In fact, it is at this point that we must turn to a view held by Levinas that is complex to the point of seeming paradoxical, and that is crucial to understanding Levinas's core insight on altruism. The question of whether altruism is possible seems to be answered thus: it is possible if we accept that it is impossible, and impossible if we accept that it is possible. But this is only an apparent contradiction. What he is saying, is that if we seek to have a free conscience, we will be forced into a soul-killing determinism. And it is only if we embrace the fact that we cannot clear our conscience that we will be freed from an absolute totalitarian judgment that finds us guilty.

That may still seem paradoxical, so here is how Levinas describes it in an essay entitled "The I and the Totality." If I seek to be certain that I have a good conscience and am innocent, I can only do so by turning to an examination of my intentions, and seeking out the forgiveness of those I have wronged. I can recognize my wrong to you, Levinas admits, "entirely in terms of my intentions" and "[h]ence the primordial value placed upon the examination of consciousness" (IT, 19). But the problem occurs when there is a third to consider. When I seek out forgiveness when there is a multiplicity of persons, I can never find everyone whom I have wronged (even for one action), because even if "I recognize my wrongs with regard to you, I may be wronging the third one through my repentance itself" (IT, 19). Repairing things with one may do harm to yet a third.[60] So even if the analysis of intentions is necessary for achieving a clear conscience, once the third arrives (and there is always a third), I can no longer find absolution. At that point, "my intention no longer exactly measures the meaning of my act" (IT, 19). As such, every intention and every action of mine becomes connected to a 'human totality.' By giving to the poor in my hometown, I am ignoring the poor in Uganda, and across the entire globe.

If I am subject to the human totality, then the only way to judge my intentions is through the abstract eyes that attempt a view of human totality. These judgments are attempted by the sociologist, the philologist, and the psychoanalyst; and under the eyes of these judgments, I become judged by the deterministic forces of history, language, and subconscious drives. In short, Levinas says, I can "be reduced to concepts" and as such, a human "becomes—not, to be sure, a thing—but a dead soul. This is history. History which is determined" (IT, 25). As such, I am reduced by psychoanalysis to either an instance of "sadism, or masochism" (IT, 31). This is the progression from seeking a clear conscience to finding oneself judged by a human totality and found with no hope of escaping the abuser/abused dichotomy. This is not unlike the analysis of Derrida that leaves us with the impossibility of neighbor-love.

What does Levinas recommend, then? If this pursuit of a pure conscience by examining our intentions leads to the loss of the human, does
Levinas suggest an alternative? Indeed, elsewhere he says that "[t]he human
is the return to the interiority of non-intentional consciousness, to bad conscience" (AT, 29). But wait. How is the return to 'bad conscience' an acceptable alternative to the impossibility of neighbor-love? In fact, how is it
different at all from declaring the impossibility of neighbor-love, other than
that we simply assume bad conscience from the beginning without waiting
and paying a psychoanalyst to give us this conclusion professionally? Did I
not conclude that Levinas was a compatibilist? How then this presupposition
of bad conscience?

Well, I should clarify what I take Levinas to mean by 'bad conscience'
(*mauvaise conscience*). By returning to bad conscience, Levinas is not declaring that he is absolutely certain of his guilt, he is simply denying the possibility of absolute certainty of his innocence. Pursuing assurance of innocence
(and thinking that such assurance is possible) entails the impossibility of
neighbor-love. But assuming the impossibility of proving myself innocent to
myself keeps me open to the possibility of actual neighbor-love. This is not
in small part what is meant by the insatiability of desire. I can never sit satiated with the knowledge that I have loved my neighbor as I am called to do.

Asymmetrical Preaching

Hopefully, the richness and depth of Levinas's understanding of asymmetrical neighbor-love is becoming more evident, as we have seen through the
negative insights of the Derrideans, and the positive insights of the compatibilists. But if Levinas's asymmetry is as described above, one may still be
inclined to side with those who accuse Levinas of speaking hyperbolically.
Does the above interpretation really account for Levinas's talk of extreme
asymmetry (without resorting to an explanation of hyperbole)?

So what justifies using such strong language, if the asymmetry he speaks
of is compatibilist as I have suggested? First of all, neighbor-love can literally
involve dying in the place of the Other, and his language suggesting this is
not hyperbolic.[61] That is enough by itself to dispel charges of hyperbole—
what greater sacrifice is there than that, after all? But there is one aspect of
this asymmetry that has been entirely missed by most of the secondary literature I have read, and under-emphasized by those that mention it. When
Levinas speaks of the asymmetry of neighbor-love, it certainly includes for
him the fact that the potentially sacrificial nature of this insatiable desire for
the Other is such that it compels him to avoid preaching it to others.

Perhaps the first mention of his allergy to preaching sacrifice comes in *Otherwise than Being*. About his ego that is involved in responsibility, he writes that it is "me and no one else." But he admits that it is 'me' who would like there to be someone returning the responsibility. It is "me with whom one would have liked to pair up a sister soul, from whom one would require substitution and sacrifice" (OB, 126). Thus, he allows that we can even hope that the Other is responsible for me in the way that I am responsible for her. But how is this asymmetrical, if I am hoping for returned responsibility? It is not bad to hope for return—it is bad to demand it. I may hope for reciprocity, "[b]ut to say that the other has to sacrifice himself to the others would be to preach human sacrifice!" (OB, 126). He does not say that there may not be such a sister soul, but he notes what it would imply for him to actually preach that to others.

In later essays and interviews, we see more frequent explanations of asymmetry in terms of preaching. He asks if we are "entering a moment in history in which the good must be loved without promises" and wonders in ink, "Perhaps it is the end of all preaching" (PO, 109). The reason for the hesitation to preach is linked to the possible lack of promises—the possible lack of reward for the sacrifice.

Elsewhere, we see this emphasized again when he states, "I can demand of myself that which I cannot demand of the other" (PM, 176). And again, the reticence to demand or preach sacrifice is connected to the lack of reward. "I would even ask whether we are not faced with an order that one cannot preach," Levinas confesses. "Does one have the right to preach to the other a piety without reward? That is what I ask myself. It is easier to tell myself to believe without promise than it is to ask it of the other. That is the idea of asymmetry" (PM, 176). That is as close to a definition as one might hope to find in the pages of Levinas. "That is the idea of asymmetry" (PM, 176).

And just to underscore that the above statements were not just the words of a preacher on a bad day, we can find him repeating the same sentiment in other places in other ways. He says of this 'for-the-Other' agapeistic relation that it "cannot give itself out as an example, or be narrated in an edifying discourse. It cannot, without becoming perverted, be made into a preachment" (US, 99). He explains why this would be perverse, noting "the outrage it would be for me to justify my neighbor's suffering" (US, 98). So clearly, a highly important factor—if not the most defining quality—of Levinas's asymmetrical relation involves an asymmetry of preaching or demand. I can demand this of myself, but how can I possibly demand it of another? The first of two interesting features of this asymmetrical preaching includes the fact that he avoids making an absolute ban on preaching—perhaps for the obvious reason that it would then be a sermon against sermonizing. He usually phrases it in terms of a question ("I would even ask . . .") or a description of his feeling about preaching ("it is easier to tell myself to believe without promise than it is to ask it of the other").[62] The second point is that when he speaks of the absence of promises, he does not absolutely deny the possibility of reward. Why is that? Perhaps it is worth a brief look into this notion of promises.

Promises, Promises

Why does Levinas, a Jew, a person of the covenant, refuse to promise the promise? It must be related, at least in part, to the fact that (writing in 1982) "This is the century that in thirty years has known two world wars, the totalitarianisms of right and left, Hitlerism and Stalinism, Hiroshima, the Gulag, and the genocides of Auschwitz and Cambodia" (US, 97) and of course, we could add Somalia, Rwanda, and others in the less than two subsequent decades. He wondered about God's silence during those times—especially during the Jewish Holocaust. And perhaps that is why he asked, as quoted earlier, if we weren't "entering a moment in history in which the good must be loved without promises" (PO, 109).

So, it is perhaps quite understandable why he would not promise the promise, especially since many of the atrocities mentioned were done in the name of one promise or another. But if Levinas was truly so pessimistic regarding the possibility of the existence of any promise, then why did he go to such lengths to avoid denying the presence of reward? He does not promise the promise but neither does he promise its absence. Could it be that Levinas had more hope than he explicitly affirmed? In another interview, Levinas again responded to the question about asymmetry, and it further supports my thesis that his asymmetry is one of asymmetrical preaching. But it gives hints of even more:

> [I]f I say that 'virtue is its own reward' I can only say so *for myself*; as soon as I make this a standard for the other I exploit him, for what I am then saying is: be virtuous towards me—work for me, love me, serve me, etc.— but don't expect anything from me in return. . . . This essential asymmetry is the very basis of ethics. (DL, 67; emphasis in original)

Again, we see him explaining his hesitancy to preach sacrifice to others. But in this case, it is in terms of virtue being its own reward. It certainly sounds as if what Levinas is describing as his own opinion is that virtue is its own reward. He definitely suggests it and does not deny it. So, is it possible that Levinas even thought that being virtuous—loving the Other with insatiable desire—was its own reward? I do not see any text in his corpus that would make us deny this possibility. And while I will not go so far as to affirm it as what Levinas actually held, I suspect that such a hope was part of Levinas's insatiable desire for the Other. The fact that he does not explicitly affirm such a promise of reward would be entirely consistent with his writing. He does not promise the promise because he is not certain of it. But he also seems to suggest that there is something inherently rewarding about being as human as possible, even if that means sacrificing to the death for another, and even if that seems irrational from certain perspectives of human nature.

But although it is muted, there is a sense of hope in the way he describes the possibility of escaping the soul-killing judgment that is allowed when one seeks a clear conscience and ends up being judged by the human totality (see discussion of 'bad conscience' earlier in this chapter). Being determined to be bound and enslaved to such a totality would be reason for despair. But he offers hope, in the form of the face of the Other. The "face breaks the system" and it is "our relationship with the . . . interlocutor . . . [that] places us above the totality" (IT, 34). He does not give us promises nor does he think we should love the Other for the sake of the promise, but he nowhere promises that there will be no reward. Given this asymmetry— given the fact that to be most fully human is to be for the Other—what more could we hope for?

Chapter 4

Levinasian Priority

La philosophie: sagesse de l'amour *au service* de l'amour

Continuing the examination of Levinas's central phrase, "philosophy is the wisdom of love at the service of love," I will now turn to the priority relationship suggested by the term 'service.' That is, I will ask how it is that wisdom is to serve love. As can be seen by looking at the way Levinas's terms interconnect,[1] we can see that the question, "How is wisdom of love to serve love?" is very similar to the question, "How is ethics to have priority over ontology?"

It is widely accepted that a central claim of Levinas's project is that ethics has priority over ontology,[2] but there is significant disagreement about what this means. Much of this disagreement can be traced to divergent interpretations of this 'priority' relationship. In this chapter, I will attempt to sort through these various interpretations, offering explanations as to where and why some of these interpretations fall short. I will also draw attention to Levinas's little-discussed distinction between 'authority' and 'power' as a distinction without which one cannot properly understand what Levinas means by this priority of ethics over ontology.

§1 Coming to Terms

For the reader less familiar with Levinas, his unique use of terminology such as 'ontology' and 'ethics' is often a source of misinterpretation. As mentioned in chapter 2, his unique nomenclature and the wide variety of terms used for similar concepts also contribute to confusion, if not indignation and

65

accusation. Therefore, I will draw upon the relevant conclusions from chapter 3 in order to proceed further with an analysis of Levinasian priority.

As I mentioned in chapter 2, the term 'ontology' is used in a way that refers to 'comprehension of being' and this applies to much of philosophy. "Western philosophy has most often been an ontology: a reduction of the other to the same by interposition of a middle and neutral term that ensures the comprehension of being" (TI, 43). Ontology is variously described as 'cognition' (TI, 43), 'thematization,' 'conceptualization' (TI, 46), 'embracing of Being' (TI, 47), 'grasping' the existent, conceptual 'possession' (TI, 46), 'reduction,' and "neutralization of the other who becomes a theme or an object" (TI, 43). Thus we can see that Levinas's use of 'ontology' refers to an epistemology of being rather than of being per se.

Levinas also uses the term 'ethics' in a unique way. In using the term 'ethics,' Levinas did not mean a set of ethical codes or an ethical theory, but rather ethics refers to the relationship between oneself and the Other. This relationship is one characterized by my responsibility for the Other, which arises out of my being called into question by the Other. This is seen when Levinas writes, "We name this calling into question of my spontaneity by the presence of the Other *ethics*" (TI, 43; my emphasis).[3]

As ontology is a 'reduction' of the Other to an object of my comprehension, ethics is the 'irreducibility' (TI, 43) of the Other to my concepts. It is this irreducibility of the Other that calls into question my attempts of reduction, and the Other's "irreducibility to . . . my thoughts and my possessions, is precisely accomplished . . . as ethics" (TI, 43). So ontology is the comprehension of being, and ethics is the responsibility for the Other, which arises out of the Other's irreducibility to my comprehension.

Ontology, as we saw in chapter 2, is tightly interlinked with other terms of wisdom such as 'justice,' 'judgment,' 'comparison,' 'measure,' 'weighing,' 'said,' 'thematization,' 'thought,' 'knowledge,' 'intelligence,' 'reason,' 'consciousness,' 'being,' 'comprehension,' 'conceptualization,' 'cognition,' 'politics,' 'the State,' 'institutions,' 'legislation,' 'law,' and 'philosophy.'

Likewise, we saw in chapter 2 that ethics or 'ethical relation' is tightly interlinked with terms of *agape* or insatiable desire such as 'metaphysical desire,' 'exteriority,' 'love without concupiscence,' 'love without *eros*,' 'love of one's neighbor,' 'conscience,' 'infinity,' 'authority,' 'saying,' 'disinterestedness,' 'responsibility,' 'revelation,' 'holiness,' 'call,' 'accusation,' 'substitution,' 'incarnation,' 'suffering,' 'sacrifice,' 'hostage,' 'persecution,' 'obsession,' 'trauma,' 'host,' 'welcome,' 'genuine freedom,' 'independence,' 'here I am,' 'attraction,' 'aspiration,' 'marvel,' 'goodness,' 'care,' 'grace,' and 'insatiable desire.'

Having laid out these terms in chapter 2, we can now turn our attention to the priority relationship itself. Drawing from these two large sets of terms, we can draw from a larger set of texts in analyzing what is meant by this priority relationship. For example, the table below highlights several of the different pairs of terms that Levinas describes as being in this prioritorial relationship.

Ethics	*has priority over*	Ontology
"Calling into question of my spontaneity by the presence of the Other"		"Comprehension of being"
Responsibility		Freedom
Other		Same
Infinity		Totality
Living-for-the-Other		Living-from-the-Other
Obsession		Possession
Metaphysics		Being
Hostage		Host
Love		Philosophy

§2 Types of Priority

I will now turn to the central aim of this chapter, which is to focus on what Levinas meant by *priority*. How is wisdom of love to *serve* love? Much turns on this question of priority, since different assessments of Levinas's project go in different directions based on how this priority is understood. For example, in certain readings of this priority in question, Levinas is said to be suggesting a mere reversal of priority, which results in the claim that Levinas's entire project is incoherent. According to the interpretations[3] that posit a mere reversal of roles, Levinas would appear to be guilty of performative self-contradiction. If, for example, one interprets Levinas's opposition to the priority of ontology (over ethics) as a rejection of 'comprehension of being' or of conceptualization, then it is clear that even as Levinas rejects conceptualization, he is doing that which he rejects. Since this notion of priority is central to Levinas's entire project, the coherence of his entire work hangs on it.

In order to address this question of Levinasian priority, I will now proceed by identifying three of the most likely candidates for types of priority—

namely a) chronological priority, b) logical priority, and c) hierarchical priority. There is evidence to suggest that any one of these priority-types might be what Levinas had in mind, yet none of these types taken in mere reversal of priority, is the type of priority Levinas defends. But he does argue for a shift in priority, so what is the locus of that shift—does it occur chronologically, logically, hierarchically? And what is the nature of that shift—is it a mere reversal, and if not, then what sort of prioritorial transformation does he suggest?

Chronological Priority

Many passages suggest that Levinas might be referring to a chronological priority of ethics over ontology. For example, Levinas writes, "responsibility for another is not an accident that happens to a subject, but *precedes* [*précède*] its essence" (OB, 114; AE, 145). Elsewhere, he uses the same temporal terminology when he writes about "substitution which precedes [précédant] the will"[4] (OB, 127; AE, 164) and again, "the critique of spontaneity [being called into question] *precedes* [*précède*] truth" (TI, 83; TeI, 55). In each of these cases, the term that precedes is closely associated with ethics. The term, 'precede' (*précéder*), is clearly a term of chronological ordering, and Levinas uses it often. Other temporal terminology is used when he writes, "the self is through and through a hostage, older [*plus anciennement*] than the ego, prior to principles" (OB, 117; AE, 150).

Elsewhere, terminology of priority is used in a way such that the context suggests temporal sequence. For example, "Responsibility for the other, this way of answering without a *prior* [*antérieure*] commitment, is human fraternity itself, and it is *prior* to freedom" (OB, 116; AE, 149). The type of chronological priority, however, that Levinas challenges is the priority of the present over the past and future. According to a classical representational view of time, the present has priority over the past and future, and the goal of knowledge is to make the past become *present* as a memory that is re-presented. Likewise, knowledge consists in the capacity to bring the future to the present and represent it as a prediction of what will at some time be present. In either case, the present is given priority in that we try to bring past and future into our present mind. It is this priority of the present that Levinas rejects. In his 1979 preface to *Time and the Other*, he asks, "Is time the very limitation of finite being or is it the relationship of finite being to God?" If we conceive of time as a "modality of finite being, time would indeed signify the dispersion of *the being of a being* into morally exclusive moments, which are, besides, as instants unstable and unfaithful even to themselves, each expelled into the past out of their own presence." In such a view of time, knowing fails because it "conceals re-presentation and reduces the *other* to presence and co-presence" (TO, 31; emphasis in original).

The responsibility that constitutes the ethical relation is not something that can be brought to the present and represented as a memory. I cannot trace my responsibility to any free choice or contract that can be remembered or brought to mind. And this is not due to the finitude of my memory, but to the fact that the origin of my responsibility is not capable of being made present in my mind. To bring something that is past to the present—in the form of a memory—is to be able to conceptualize the past as a presence or as ontological thought. But since the ethical relation comes before ontology, in a sense, it comes before conceivable time. As Adriaan Peperzak explained Levinas's view, "Not being able to be the origin of my responsibilities and obligations—not even by a reflection in the style of Plato's remembrance—I am aware that the past from which I stem is more past than any past that can be recalled to memory."[5] As Levinas writes in a later essay, the "past is irreducible to the present" (PT, 32).

Neither, however, does Levinas advocate viewing the future in terms of the present. Our relation to the future is one that is "contrasting strongly with the synchronizable time of re-presentation" (TO, 114). Our relation to the future is not merely making the future fully present. This dwelling in 'pure future,' which he opposes, is a dwelling on 'promises' (DR, 177) or a being "preoccupied with ultimate ends" (DR, 176). This formal view of time would have us bring the future to the present.

Levinas denounces the possibility, or even the desirability, of the goal of representational philosophy—that is, to "wrest from the past and the future . . . a presence, already or still ungraspable, or the past or the yet to come" (PT, 13). It is not hard to see that Levinas rejects this representational view of time and the priority of the present over the past or over the future. The far more difficult problem, however, is discerning what sort of priority he suggests in lieu of this present-centric view of time. *Is it a mere reversal, whereby the past or future has priority over the present? Is it a demolition of any sort of priority? Or is it a challenge to the terms of that very question?*

Looking at the first option of 'mere reversal' of priority over present, it may seem plausible that Levinas suggests that we make the past or future our primary concern, giving either past or future a priority over the present. But how would such a role-reversal lead us beyond the tyranny of synchrony? It is clear that Levinas addresses the problem in terms of *diachrony* rather than in terms of *synchrony*. Viewing time in terms of synchrony grants the isolated moment ultimate significance. As such, the question of priority viewed in terms of synchrony seeks to find which *moment* has priority: the present moment, a moment in the past, or a moment in the future? If we see diachrony as the answer to the problem raised by the question of synchrony, then we will never escape the synchronic paradigm. Instead of answering the question with diachrony, Levinas seeks to ask a different question altogether.

All these answers (priority of presence, priority of past, or priority of future) accept the premise of the synchronous question—namely they all give significance to an instant in time. The synchrony of representational time sees "temporality taken as the flow of instants" (PT, 31). Viewing time diachronically, however, sets aside the goal of bringing all to one solitary moment (either past, present, or future).

In contrast to the synchrony that seeks to conjoin the past with the present or the future with the present, "diachrony is the refusal of conjunction" and is in "this sense, infinite" (OB, 11). As presence and synchrony are strongly linked to totalization, so diachrony is a relation to the infinite. Diachrony is an "irreducible divergency that opens here between the non-present and every representable divergency" (OB, 10–11). In seeking a way to replace the priority of the moment, we are thus called to view the priority in terms of diachrony, which is a relation between the present and that which is beyond the present (either past or future). However, not just any sort of relationship of present and future will do. To give a diachronic, relational answer to the question of which moment is of primary importance does not break free from the tyranny of the moment. If synchrony is a totalizing absorption of the future by the present, its mere reversal does not escape totalization, either. In the preface to *Time and the Other*, Levinas writes that diachrony is not the absorption of the infinite other by the present 'Same': this is merely a "relationship without relation." Diachrony, however, is not the mere reversal of this absorption. To replace the absorption of the infinite future by the present with the absorption of the present by the infinite is 'ecstasis' which he also rejects (TO, 35). Either type of absorption destroys the relation, and either type of priority is totalizing. If, then, the priority relation is not merely a reversal that makes the infinite swallow up the present, what alternatives are there?

Another alternative is to suggest that there should be a destruction of priority altogether. Instead of giving priority to the future, past or present, one could say that all moments are mutually and equally significant. Levinas, in fact, says that his is "not a gratuitous or vain quest for some kind of chronological priority" (AT, 174). This means he is not seeking a chronological priority in terms of synchrony where either the future, the past, or the present must have some privilege. But even this response which seeks to level out all moments as having the same importance assumes the framing of the question in terms of isolated moments and denies the possibility of the past to address the present or the present to be challenged by the future. Denying synchrony, though, is not simply to deny time. To deny temporality entirely amounts to "insanity and an absurd anachronism" (TO, 34). To turn from synchrony to diachrony, however, is not simply a denial of time. It is tempting to say that the diachronous time is simply a negative concept that consists in the absence of coincidence or absorption (in either direction). But the "impossibility of coinciding . . . [is] not simply [a] negative notion" (TO, 32).

The emphasis, rather, is upon a relation—the "always of the relationship." It is a "relationship that is different from all the other relationships of our logic and psychology" (TO, 32). Even though the relationship is often described by what it is not, it is a relationship in time that is not merely a limit.

We might desire to escape time, seeing it as a limitation and a painful reminder of our finitude. But Levinas asks, "Is time the very limitation of the finite being, or is it the relationship of finite being to God?" (TO, 32). He is not rejecting time and embracing anachronism. Our being in time does not keep us from encountering the infinite, but is the very condition in which we can relate to the infinite.

So when Levinas challenges the priority of ontology over ethics, is he speaking of a chronological priority? In a way, yes. But it is not a reversal of priority (where the absorption is now switched). The "past is irreducible to the present" (PT, 32), but the present is also irreducible to the past or future. There is no pure coincidence. Neither, however, is it a denial of chronology altogether. The sort of time Levinas points to is transcendent time—time which is a diachronic, temporal, nonreductive relation.

Logical Priority

There are also many passages suggesting that the priority Levinas has in mind is logical priority. Without immediately defining what is meant by this logical priority, I will first point to the fact that Levinas speaks of logical priority. Levinas clearly seeks to challenge the view that ontology has logical priority over ethics, and this can be seen in many comments, such as when Levinas writes that "theology imprudently . . . presupposes the *logical privilege* of totality" (TI, 293; my emphasis).

Furthermore, he writes in the conclusions of *Totality and Infinity*, "Social relations do not simply present us with a superior empirical matter, to be treated in terms of the logic of genus and species" (290). That Levinas critiqued this logical priority of ontology over ethics is uncontroversial, but the more difficult question is whether Levinas also suggested a simple reversal of logical priority, such that ethics ought to have a simple logical priority over ontology.

There are passages that could be used to argue that a mere reversal of logical priority is indeed what Levinas suggested. "The one-for-the-other," says Levinas, "is the *foundation* of theory, for it *makes possible* relationship" (OB, 136). This seems to suggest that the ethical relation is the logical foundation, in the sense that the ethical relation is the logical condition of possibility for ontology. This also seems to be the case when we read that, "truth is *founded* on relationship with the other" (TI, 99). Again, we find it simply put that "ontology *presupposes* metaphysics" (TI, 48).

Despite the appearance of a mere reversal of logical priority, such an interpretation is denied by Levinas in many different ways. One could read that "obsession is an accusation *without foundation*" (OB, 110), and simply conclude that the ethical relation is the a priori foundation of ontology, but would then be faced with the explicit rejections of such a priority. "A neighbor," Levinas writes, "concerns me *outside of every a priori*. But perhaps before every a priori, or from an earlier moment than that of the a priori" (OB, 192 n. 20). Elsewhere, we read, "what is prior to every question is *not* . . . *knowledge* possessed *a priori*" (TI, 177). Furthermore, in the conclusions of *Totality and Infinity*, Levinas summarizes, "This work has not sought to describe the psychology of the social relation . . . definitively in formal logic" (289).

Thus, it appears that Levinas is at some points speaking as if ethics has a logical priority over ontology, while at other points he is simply denying that the priority in question is a logical priority. This leaves Levinas in a possibly precarious position. He is clearly not suggesting that philosophy proceed as normal with ontology having logical priority over ethics. But neither is he suggesting a mere reversal of priority. The option of a flat rejection of logic altogether is also ruled out on account of his frequent usage of logical terms and concepts. His philosophy is either blatantly self-contradictory, or there is another way to understand this priority relationship. I would like to suggest the latter.

While it may seem contradictory to use logical foundational terminology when discussing priority while simultaneously denying the logical nature of this priority, this can be explained by noting that the logical priority in question is foundational in the sense that it is an epistemological priority. That is, A is logically prior to B in that B is derived from A. In order for me to make logical inferences from A to B, however, it requires that I comprehend A. In this way, one could say that the ethical relation, even though it is logically prior to ontology, is not such that it can be completely comprehended, because the Other, by definition, is irreducible to that which can be comprehended. Since it cannot be comprehended, one cannot make logical inferences from it. Might it be, then, that this accounts for the language of logical priority while still denying the ability to derive logical conclusions from the ethical relation?

Luk Bouckaert points to an important factor of this priority relation when he emphasizes the epistemic implications of Levinas's priority relation. He argues that the emphasis is upon the order of epistemic access, as is seen when he says, "The philosophical significance of Levinas's critique of Heidegger lies in this rejection of ontological thinking as ultimate relation to reality." And he is mostly accurate when he claims that "Levinas's fundamental endeavour is to question Heidegger's ontological way of thinking itself and to submit it to a new experience, whose starting point is no longer the Self but the Other." He is accurate, because the central epistemological point is that the self is no longer the epistemic starting point. But Bouckaert is only *mostly* accurate since one cannot say that the Other is the starting point in the same way that the self used to be the epistemic starting point. Levinas denies that one can derive conclusions from the Other as if the Other were an a priori principle for the following simple reason: the Other cannot be reduced to a principle. To interpret Levinas in this simple reversal of logical foundations leads to the conclusion that he is self-contradictory, and that explains why Bouckaert, in fact, arrives at the conclusion that Levinas is finally in contradiction with himself. He says that Levinas does not succeed in avoiding the type of logical, ontological thinking he seeks to avoid. Bouckaert concludes that Levinas's thinking "[does] not contain a transcending of ontological thinking."[6]

It is safe to say, as Bouckaert does, that for Levinas, nothing is logically prior to the ethical relation, but Bouckaert misses an important qualification. The fact that the ethical relation has no logical antecedents does not imply that the ethical relation itself is the logical antecedent from which we can draw ontological conclusions. To say that the ethical relation is the logical antecedent to ontology would imply the possibility of comprehending the antecedent such that we could derive conclusions from it, but in fact, Levinas denies our ability to comprehend the antecedent. Therefore, rather than saying that the ethical relation is the first term in a system of comprehensible terms and conditional relations between those terms, Levinas holds that the ethical relation is prior to the system itself.

By positioning ethics prior to logic, Levinas is not suggesting that it is opposed to logic or contrary to the laws of induction. When speaking about responsibility as the foundation of freedom, Levinas explains that "to be without a choice can seem to be violence only to an abusive or hasty and imprudent reflection, for it precedes the freedom non-freedom couple" (OB, 116). He is not embracing the illogical, but is pointing to the prelogical. He speaks of the ethical responsibility for the Other as that which is prior to our ability to make comprehensible logical derivations or choices.

To explain Levinas's inversion of logical priority more fully, one is helped by considering the logical priority suggested by Husserl or Heidegger, since Levinas's rejection of ontological priority over ethics is largely developed as a rejection of the Husserlian and Heideggerian onto- logical privilege. Looking at the Husserlian mode of ontological philoso- phizing, Theodorus de Boer writes that "[t]o philosophize is to trace freedom back to what lies before it," and Husserl's transcendental phe- nomenology "belongs to the age-old philosophical tradition of seeking a foundation in the self, in immanent perception, in the for-itself of con- sciousness."[7] This is the type of philosophizing that Levinas calls 'egoism' or 'narcissism' and to which Levinas seeks an alternative.

I like to describe this alternative as a "prolegomena to any future ethical theory,"[8] drawing a parallel to Kant in that this ethical relation is that which comes prior to any encounter but is not itself encountered. It is not some Platonic experience that the soul now recollects. Rather, as de Boer puts it, the "condition for experience is not itself experienced." This helps disam- biguate the possible confusion that arises when one considers the logical pri- ority of ethics over ontology. Levinas is not saying that an ethical theory is prior to ontology. But rather the fact of my being infinitely 'for-the-other' is prior to any ethical theory. Levinas seeks the "source behind the source" and instead of finding it in the self, as Husserl does, he finds it in the "condition behind the condition."[9]

De Boer cuts through much of the confusion by drawing attention to the 'condition behind the condition.' But what is that condition? Does Levinas identify that, 'condition behind the condition' as the Other as de Boer suggests?[10]

The problem as de Boer sees it is that if we say, like Buber, that 'I become through Thou' and this is meant as a metaphysical statement, then we are faced with the dilemma of origins. We cannot say that the I existed prior to engagement with the Other since the engagement with the other is what constitutes the I. Even if we say that the Other and I are 'mutually con- stitutive,' the Thou must already be, but "this Thou cannot be unless an I constitutes it, etc." There must be a distinct I and Thou before the I can be constituted by the Thou. De Boer attempts to solve this problem by suggesting that I am not "'constituted' by the Other, for in my joyous existence I already was an independent being." Rather, suggests de Boer, in the "encounter with the other a transformation from egoism to altruism takes place." In this encounter, "I am awakened to responsibility."[11] This solution may appear to solve the problem above, but it creates a larger problem by locating the metaphysical origin of the self within the self (as of yet detached from the Other) and to make the role of the Other secondary to the primordial self. What Levinas suggests is far more radical than that. Levinas posits the Other as having a primordial constitutive role in the I.

Levinas points to the "self as . . . prior to activity and passivity" (OB, 116). Self and the responsibility which constitutes self is neither actively chosen nor passively accepted. Self occurs "without choice" and is "without a prior commitment" (OB, 116). Rather, it is a "passivity beneath all passivity" (OB, 101, 115). Awareness of the responsibility may come later, but the responsibility (and thus oneself) exists prior to that awareness. "To be oneself, otherwise than being, . . . is to bear the wretchedness and bankruptcy of the other" (OB, 117).

The condition behind the condition *exists* in the Other—it is not merely an awareness, though the awareness that occurs is vital. "I exist through the other and for the other" (OB, 114). Of course, this sounds like it is a mere reversal of the logical priority of ontology over ethics. It seems to make me completely derivable from the Other in a way that negates the self. The ethical relation with the Other is the "prolegomena to any future ethics" without but the Other is not a principle from which my ego is derived. More concrete examples of this will follow the treatment of hierachical priority of the ethical relation over ontology. It is that to which I shall now turn.

Hierarchical Priority

There is strong evidence that the type of priority Levinas speaks of is related to hierarchical priority. And because of the fact that the priority is not chronological or logical, strictly speaking, it is all the more likely that the priority in question is a hierarchical one. By hierarchical priority, I mean a relationship in which one term is dominated by another such that the one with hierarchical priority rules the Other and if the two are in conflict, the one with priority is determinative. Levinas objects to the way in which ontology is usually viewed as having a dominating role over the ethical relation to the Other. For example, Levinas declares, "If ontology—the comprehension . . .

of Being—is impossible . . . it is because the comprehension of Being in general cannot *dominate* the relationship with the Other" (TI, 47; emphasis in original).

The priority Levinas seeks to overturn is the *dominating* priority of ontology which knows no limits. This overpowering priority is described when Levinas writes that "sovereign reason knows only itself, [and] that nothing limits it" (TI, 43). The important message is that the relationship with the Other cannot ultimately be at the service of ontology. Levinas writes, "Responsibility for the others has not been a return to oneself, but an exasperated contracting, which the limits of identity cannot retain" (OB, 114). This reveals Levinas viewing ontology as an insufficient ruler of the responsibility for the Other. But does he go beyond that to suggest that ontology should be ruled by that very ethical relationship? If reason dominated with an iron fist, what sort of reversal of authority is Levinas suggesting that the responsibility for the Other exercises over reason? It seems that he might be suggesting that we replace a tyrant with a tyrant, when he suggests that the Other be one's master. For example, "the Other as master can also serve us as an example of an alterity that is . . . visible only from an I" (TI, 121). So then, is one domineering master to be replaced by its slave, merely switching roles and establishing another master/slave domination? Some have interpreted him to be suggesting just that. For example, Ricoeur sees Levinas as positing the Other as "a master of justice . . . [who] forbids murder and commands justice."[12] This is not what Levinas says, however, since Levinas draws our attention to the face which is *not* a mere revolt which turns reason on its head—"the metaphysical other . . . is not the simple reverse of identity, and is not formed out of resistance to the same" (TI, 38).

Levinas submits that the "ethical relation, opposed to first philosophy which identifies freedom and power, is not contrary to truth" (TI, 47). The ethical relation is not contrary to truth, but he just aims to put first philosophy (ontology) in its place. It is not first place, but what place is it? We know that it is limited somehow by the responsibility of the ethical relationship, but how? We may be surprised to read that "in the incomparable relationship of responsibility, the other no longer limits the same, [but] it is supported by what it limits" (OB, 115). If the same is now supporting the Other (rather than just being limited by it), then the subordination of ontology to ethics looks to be a kinder, gentler relation.

We can conclude that it is not as simple as a mere role reversal of domination. We cannot say that it is a simple hierarchical priority in the way that ontology has enjoyed dominance over the ethical relation. How, then, do we understand this hierarchical priority, and is it even coherent?

§3 The Gyges Test

Now that I have narrowed the understanding of priority to 'hierarchical priority' of some kind, I will turn (in §4 of this chapter) to four different ways of interpreting whether and how Levinas thought that hierarchical priority of ontology over ethics ought to be overturned. Before examining these various interpretations, however, I will offer what can serve as an interpretive test for each of these views. By attending to what I think is Levinas's paradigmatic myth—the myth of Gyges—we can see certain features of the priority relationship that Levinas is establishing and other features which he seeks to avoid. The importance of this myth (which I first mentioned in chapter 1) in Levinas's work is evident in the frequency with which he alludes to Gyges (TI, 61, 90, 170, 173, 221–22; OB, 113, 118, 145, 149).[13] It is also important since he uses it to refer to the central notion of priority.

As it is found in Plato's *Republic*,[14] the myth of Gyges tells of a man who takes a ring from an entombed skeleton. He later discovers that when he turns the ring's collet toward himself, the ring makes him invisible to others, even while others remain visible to him. Discovering this trick, he uses it to seduce the queen, kill the king, and set himself up as tyrant. Levinas points us to this myth when he says, "The myth of Gyges is the very myth of the I . . . which exist[s] non-recognized" (TI, 61). To be nonrecognized is to be free from the accusation of the Other while being free to accuse others as one sees fit, and it enables one to exercise a dominating authority over others.

In Levinas's use of this myth, sight is analogous to cognition and language—cognition which conceptualizes the Other in categories of thought and speech that accuse the Other. The cognitive aspect of Gyges' sight is apparent in the following passage. When one "see[s] without being seen, like Gyges" it is "a determination of the other by the same, without the same being determined by the other" (TI, 170). Gyges' asymmetrical conceptual 'determination'[15] is associated with "a total reflection—which cognition aims at" (TI, 221). The linguistic character of Gyges' sight is seen when Levinas writes, "Gyges plays a double game . . . speaking to 'others' and evading speech" (TI, 173). Gyges can accuse while evading accusation.

Sight, which is analogous to an asymmetrical cognition of the Other, is also related to ethical responsibility, as is seen when Levinas writes that rather than being conceptualized and limited by the Other, one would prefer, like Gyges, "to take refuge in one's concept in which the limits of obligation are found" (GDT, 196). Concepts are thus used in an attempt to limit or eliminate the obligation that I have for the Other, and the effect of cognitive invisibility to others is ethical immunity to the command of the Other. The condition of Gyges is the "eventuality of all unpunished crimes," and this impunity is related to being 'non-recognized'[16] (TI, 61). Elsewhere, Levinas describes "Gyges' position" as having both the moral trait of 'impunity' and the cognitive trait of 'certitude' (TI, 90).

This myth captures the very ontological structure (TI, 170) that Levinas seeks to overturn. The myth expresses the conceptual nature of the type of ontology Levinas opposes as well as the ethical consequences[17] of embracing such an ontology, and most importantly, it sheds light on his view of the priority relationship between ontology and ethics. Levinas's frequent use of the myth invites the reader to use it to aid in understanding how and why Levinas opposed the priority of ontology over ethics. I will use it for that purpose, but I will also use it for the more difficult task of understanding what sort of priority Levinas suggested replace the priority of ontology over ethics.

Levinas opposes this totalizing cognition that reduces others to one's concepts but hides from the conceptualization and accusation of the Other. But does Levinas oppose the gaze of Gyges to the point of opposing sight altogether? If he did, then in these metaphoric terms I have just described, he would be recommending blindness. If a mere reversal of the totalizing Gyges was Levinas's ideal, then he would have advocated blind exposure—being seen without seeing. But Levinas did no such thing; instead, he warned against this mere reversal. Those who oppose all thought in the effort to avoid totalizing thought would be making the error of having a "foundation of pluralism" (OB, 221). Opposing totality on the foundation of pluralism (the opposition to totality) would be to make the opposition to theory one's theme. This would be to become "statues looking at one another with empty eyes, idols which, contrary to Gyges, are exposed and do not see" (TI, 222). Levinas clearly wants to resist Gyges' invisible gaze, but not by becoming a blind statue.

The totalizing[18] gaze of Gyges, since it implied a rejection of responsibility to the other, was a form of violence that Levinas opposed. But what did he embrace instead? He was insistent that the peace he sought could not be defined merely in terms of a rejection of violence. The "exclusion of violence," Levinas explained, "by beings susceptible of being integrated into a totality is not equivalent to peace" (TI, 222).

Levinas used phrases such as "breaking open the secret of Gyges" (BPW, 104) and "being torn away from the secret of Gyges" (BPW, 105), so it is clear that whatever this secret of Gyges is, it can be broken. It is not just some impossible ideal that is never achieved, but is something that he repeatedly speaks of as that which can be actualized.

What is the ontological priority that hides Gyges? What is the way to break that secret? And what model of priority did he suggest replace it? Those will be the questions I pursue throughout this chapter. Levinas's use of the Gyges myth cannot provide us with detailed answers to those questions, but it can help identify what range of answers Levinas sought to give, and it can serve to dismiss, refine, or confirm possible interpretations of those answers. This Gyges test is especially helpful in revealing which interpretations are *not* correct, because not only does he clearly oppose the priority of ontology over ethics, but he also rejects any type of priority that is a mere reversal of priority. This test can also help direct the inquiry toward what sort of priority he thought was the alternative. One key feature this replacement priority will have is that of achievability. Whatever priority Levinas spoke of, it is clear that he did not see it as an impossible ideal, so any interpretation that views Levinas as endorsing such a view must also be dismissed.

§4 Assessments

Having dealt with the apparently contradictory talk of chronological and logical priority, I will now turn to the problems involved with taking this priority to be hierarchical. I will do so by examining some of the secondary literature to identify four distinct ways that the conflicting evidence (about hierarchical priority) is handled. Three of these responses to the apparent contradictions help identify interpretations to be avoided, while the fourth offers the most promise for a faithful understanding of Levinas on this point of priority. This fourth option, even though it is probably the most accurate interpretation, may nonetheless be difficult to accept as plausible. I will then draw attention to a crucial and uncommon distinction made by Levinas, which is necessary for granting the plausibility of the position.

Incoherent Reversal of Priority

One of the four responses to the apparent contradictions in Levinas's work is to simply conclude that they are in fact performatively self-contradictory. Those taking this view see Levinas as suggesting a mere reversal of priority, and on that basis accuse him of self-contradiction. This view finds that in *making the claim* that ontology or language is violent, Levinas himself engages in language and thus partakes in the very violence he uses language to oppose. Derrida criticizes Levinas on this point in "Violence and Metaphysics," insisting that language and conceptualization are inherently violent. The nonviolent language that Levinas seeks is impossible according to Derrida, precisely because language begins as violence and is necessarily violent. Thus Derrida writes that Levinas must accept the fact that "pure nonviolence is a contradictory concept."[19]

Derrida opposes the violence of philosophy (language and thought) but nonetheless thinks we must embrace the fact that "[i]f one has to philosophize, one has to philosophize; if one does not have to philosophize, one still has to philosophize (to say it and think it). One always has to philosophize." Then he adds, as if to admit surprise that Levinas would make this mistake, "Levinas knows this better than others."[20]

Despite the inherent violence of language and thought, the alternative Derrida argues is that even though language in its essence is violence, it still can be put to nonviolent purposes. "Nonviolence would be the *telos*," says Derrida, "and not the essence of discourse." In this way, language is always violent, but some violence is better than other violence, in that some language is "violence against violence."[21] Using 'light' metaphorically to represent language and thought,[22] Derrida posits that "[i]f light is the element of violence, one must combat light with a certain other light, in order to avoid the worst violence, the violence of the night which precedes or represses discourse." What Derrida means by the 'worst violence' is more evident in the following comment about the lesser of two evils: "The philosopher . . . *must* speak and write within this war of light, a war in which he always already knows himself to be engaged; a war which he knows is inescapable, except by denying discourse, that is, by risking the worst violence." The only way to achieve pure nonviolence, according to Derrida, would be to deny discourse (which is necessarily violent), but for Derrida, the denial of discourse is the "worst violence." Less violent than the worst violence is to "tend toward justice by acknowledging and practicing the violence within [language]."[23]

Derrida and others who take this view have characterized Levinas's priority of ethics over ontology as nonviolence that is defined by the absence of violence. In the Gyges model, this would be to say that Levinas's opposition to the priority of ontology over ethics amounted to the opposite of Gyges who is an unseen seer. Derrida's interpretation has Levinas advocating opposition to all sight, leading to the ideal of blindness. This interpretation fails the Gyges test since, as I have shown, Levinas's ideal is *not* a mere reversal of Gyges' position. Recall that Levinas opposed the reverse model, which is the blind statue. When explaining why the statue—the reversal of Gyges—is also to be avoided, he says, "the exclusion of violence by beings susceptible of being integrated into a totality is not equivalent to peace" (TI, 222). The absence of violence may be good, but peace, according to Levinas, is not merely defined negatively.

If Levinas did suggest that all language and theorizing was violent, and that the way to peace was simply to oppose this violence, then Levinas would be subject to the charge of performative contradiction. But I am arguing that Levinas did not make such a claim. Derrida interprets Levinas's critique of ontological priority over ethics to be a call for the reversal of priority, and concludes that it is impossible for a reversal to yield peace, since such a reversal would yield the worst violence of all—the absence of discourse and the resultant isolation. I am arguing that whatever Levinas meant by this pacific ethical relation, it is clear that he did not mean a mere reversal of violence— a mere absence of violence. Derrida's criticism of Levinas is instructive, however, since it helps us see what Levinas is not saying, and what consequences would follow if he *did* say it. My purpose here, nonetheless, is to discover what Levinas did say about priority, so to understand what type of priority Levinas was embracing, we will have to turn elsewhere.

Coherent Reversal of Priority

Another response to Levinas's apparently contradictory statements about priority is similar to Derrida's in that it identifies Levinas's pacific ethical relation with the avoidance of violence (avoidance of all language). But it parts from Derrida by concluding that this silence is what we must embrace. As we just observed, Derrida described silence—the silence that results from denying discourse—as the worst violence. The type of assessment I am describing here, however, interprets Levinas as having rejected ontology so thoroughly that the only way to respond is by avoiding theorizing altogether. This view can be seen in the passages below by John Llewelyn.[24]

Writing on Levinas's priority of ethics over ontology, Llewelyn concluded his essay confessing with near exasperation, "When Derrida and Levinas have begun deconstructing the ontic metaphors of priority . . . we can expect to have difficulty deciding what or who is prior to what or whom." The concluding sentence of Llewelyn's essay on Levinas's priority relation admits, "When faced with the question whether ontology is beyond metaphysics or metaphysics is beyond being, we may *be at a loss for words*."[25]

To suggest that a loss of words is the way to lose the violence of ontology is an attempt to preserve the coherence of Levinas's position. To say that philosophical silence is the only way to achieve this nonviolence is to achieve coherence at the cost of nihilism. Derrida chose to embrace the contradiction of using 'violence against violence' only because it was better than the 'worst violence' of nihilism or absolute mystical silence.[26] If one understands language to be inherently violent, and takes nonviolence to be the mere absence of language, then one can either embrace the contradiction in order to avoid absolute silence, or accept absolute silence in order to avoid incoherence. Derrida chose the former option, and this second interpretive view is the choice of the latter option, but both views share the common presupposition that language is inherently violent, and that pure nonviolence is the absence of language.

Even though this second view allows Levinas to come out holding a coherent view, it nonetheless is not an interpretation Levinas would welcome. Like the first view, it misinterprets Levinas's ideal of nonviolence and fails the Gyges test, since it attributes to Levinas an ideal which Levinas rejects—namely the ideal of the blind statue, the absence of language. This second view differs from the former view only in that it is willing to embrace that ideal, while Derrida is not.

Levinas saw his view as neither incoherent nor as embracing absolute silence, so both of these first two options must be ruled out. I now turn to a third view, which avoids both of these shortcomings but fails for another reason.

Mutuality of Priority

A third response to the apparent contradictions in Levinas's treatment of priority is to rescue Levinas from incoherence by suggesting that the priority is not a true priority but one in which the *relata* are mutually correcting. This third interpretation of Levinas does not charge him with either performative self-contradiction (like the first interpretation) or with absolute silence (like the second), and avoids these problems by suggesting that instead of a true priority where one term has priority over the Other, both terms are of equal priority. Consider, for example, Jamie Ferreira's recent article on Levinas's priority of responsibility over freedom.[27] In it, she defends Levinas against the criticism that he grants such a dominant priority of responsibility over freedom that it does not allow for moral agency.

In this excellent piece, Ferreira rightly argues, contrary to the first two views just discussed, that Levinas is not just advocating a reversal of priority. "Levinas's response to what he sees as the excessive emphasis on individual autonomy," Ferreira writes, "is more nuanced than the mere substitution of heteronomy." It is from the standpoint of this position that she is able to say, "It is (I hope) a commonplace by now that Levinas's account does not preclude the possibility of justice."[28] But what is the nuance in interpretation that allows her to make this claim? Like several others who interpret Levinas this way—allowing mutual priority—she recognizes that the origin of language and thought arises out of the encounter with 'the third.'

In order to explain the importance of the third in this interpretation of Levinas, I should briefly describe its role in Levinas's work. The ethical relation involves just two—'I' (*le Moi*) and the 'Other' (*Autrui*)—but when another 'Other' comes on the scene, this is 'the Third' (*le Tiers*).[29] I am infinitely responsible to the Other and Levinas says this responsibility is "certainly prior to all questions." But "a third party disturbs that exteriority of two people" (PP, 142) and this affects my unique obligation to the Other, because once 'the third' arrives, I must now split my obligation between the Other and the third. "The third party is other than the neighbour but also another neighbour." This causes me to ask, "What am I to do? What have they already done to one another? Which comes before the Other in my responsibility?" Thus the third is the "Birth of the question" which requires that I violate the incomparability of the Other and begin "a weighing, a calculation, the comparison of incomparables" (PP, 142).

This view is in contrast to theories of original hostility, such as Hobbes's, which describe humans as naturally at war and which has language and justice arising as a limitation of that violence. Levinas, on the other hand, describes an ego naturally obligated to the Other and has language and justice arising as a limitation of that initial infinite obligation.

As Levinas says quite clearly, "Consciousness is born as the presence of 'the third' party in the proximity of the one to the other" (PP, 144). He says even more explicitly in *Otherwise than Being* that "The fact that the other, my neighbor, is also a third party with respect to another, who is also a neighbor, is the birth of thought, consciousness, justice and philosophy" (128).

The importance of the third is perhaps less pronounced in the earlier *Totality and Infinity*, but as Peter Atterton argues,[30] Derrida misread Levinas on precisely this point, ignoring the fact that Levinas located the birth of language not simply in the original ethical relation (between the I and the Other) but in the introduction of the third into the ethical relation.[31] To read Levinas in a way that ignores this leads to one of the interpretive options of 'reversal' I have described in the sections "Incoherent Reversal of Priority" and "Coherent Reversal of Priority" above. Atterton shows the pivotal importance of the third when he writes, "Were one to affirm the double originality of language *without* reference to the third party—as Derrida himself does—arguably one would have to abandon the idea of establishing an order of priority . . . altogether."[32]

It is no surprise then, that each of the interpretations that suggest Levinas allowed for a mutual priority also recognizes that he located the birth of language in the introduction of the third.[33] This 'mutuality' interpretation has the advantage over the first two 'reversal' interpretations in that it has overwhelming evidence on its side regarding the role of the third. This allows these mutuality positions to view Levinas as holding a coherent position. There is, however, another problem that the mutuality interpretations face—namely, even though an equal mutuality is easier to accept because of its coherence, how does this mutuality account for the radical asymmetry (even after the introduction of the third) that is so adamantly emphasized throughout Levinas's *oeuvre*?

Let us take a closer look at the mutual priority as it is suggested by Ferreira. 'Hostage' is a term for this prevolitional responsibility, but Levinas also uses the term 'host' which allows for the moral agent to 'welcome' freely the responsibility for the Other. Ferreira summarized the priority of the host and the hostage by saying, "'[h]ost' and 'hostage' are *mutually correcting* tropes."[34] By focusing on the welcome of the Other, Ferreira rightly shows one Levinasian way of encountering the ethical relation such that the free-dom of the moral agent is maintained. She is right to note the two contrast-ing encounters—the gentle or 'discreet' encounter as a host of the Other, and the hostile or 'indiscreet' encounter of being taken hostage by the Other. But can we accurately say that Levinas saw these as "mutually correcting tropes" such that one always has recourse to the welcome of the host to counter the violence of being taken hostage? If these truly were mutually correcting tropes, then my role as a host would sometimes be in a position to 'correct' the one taking me hostage. That would be to say that I am in a symmetrical relationship with the Other such that I can sometimes correct the authority of the Other. Is that indeed Levinas's view?

I find it tempting to take such a view—a view that is also defended by Burggraeve. He, too, takes into consideration the third and thereby avoids the problems encountered in the Derridean readings. However, he responds to the third by suggesting this entrance now places me on 'equal footing' with all others. Burggraeve, for example, says that "with the appearance of the third, symmetry enters proximity" and that "we stand equally before one another." This new situation of equal standing "makes reciprocity possible."[35]

I find it difficult to see that Levinas endorsed such a model of mutual-ity that would allow for me—within the ethical relation—to demand that the Other be responsible for me in this sacrificial way. This denies the abso-lute authority or 'height' that the Other has over me and the radical asym-metry that is essential to the ethical relation—an asymmetry which does not completely disappear with the appearance of the third. If we were to apply the Gyges test to this interpretation, it would do well on two counts, but would ultimately fall short. This account of mutuality is avoiding both extremes by the test—it avoids the unseen seer (since this model allows the Other to see me) and it avoids the unseeing seen statues that simply oppose all sight (since this model allows for language and theory). The problem with this account is that it does not accurately describe the way in which Gyges' secret is broken.

This model suggests that Gyges shares the secret with others, and that in doing so, Gyges maintains an ability (now mitigated by his voluntary disclosure) to 'correct' the Other's authority—a lighter sentence in exchange for a guilty plea, if you will. In fact, however, this is not how the secret is revealed. As Levinas describes it, the secret is "broken open." I am "torn away from Gyges' secret" (TDT, 104, 105). These do not sound like plea bargains, and especially not in the case where being torn from Gyges' secret is described as being "'taken by the hair' from the bottom of my obscurity" (OB, 149). The way the secret-breaking is described emphasizes its *in*-voluntariness. Whatever degree of choice may or may not be present by including the notion of the welcome, one thing that is clear is that there is no mutuality between 'being chosen' and 'choosing.' Being chosen precedes my volition, as is made clear when Levinas says that the Good, which inclines me toward responsibility, "chooses me *before* I welcome it" (OB, 123; my emphasis). Therefore, ascribing a model of mutuality to Levinas ultimately fails the Gyges test for its failure to grant the asymmetrical authority of the Other which breaks my secret before I welcome it.

Further evidence that the welcome does not mitigate the authority of the Other over me is found when Levinas compares the welcome of the Other to Buber's I-Thou relation: "The Other who welcomes in intimacy is not the *you* [*vous*] of the face that reveals itself in a dimension of height, but precisely the *thou* [*tu*] of familiarity," which is the Thou of the "I-Thou [presented by] Buber" (TI, 155; emphasis in the original). Even though Levinas was influenced by him, Levinas nonetheless rejects Buber's "I-Thou" relation as the model for the ethical relation precisely because it is too symmetrical or mutual.[36]

Ferreira speaks of the two realms in Levinas's ethics: the realm of the ethical relation, which is the realm of infinite personal responsibility, and the realm where there is equity and mutuality. Since the realm of personal responsibility only occurs when there is not yet a third, and since there is always a third,[37] she concludes, "Levinas does not require a stark contrast between a pure realm of personal responsibility and a pure realm of justice." Ferreira sums this view saying that Levinas's "admission that there never is a case in which 'the third' is not involved reestablishes a single realm, which could be called either the realm of love or justice." The problem with collapsing the two realms is that it effectively eliminates the priority that love is supposed to have over justice. She anticipates my objection, asking how "can we keep the counterweight of infinite responsibility in the face of justice's limits on self-sacrifice?" and admits that the only way "to respond to this potential objection is to say that Levinas maintains his view of justice *in tension* with his view of infinite responsibility."[38] This tension she describes is nonetheless an equal tension, which I believe belies the priority of the infinite responsibility.

This mutuality view is also represented when William Paul Simmons says, "Although the Third universalizes the an-archical relationship with the Other into the political realm, it does not supplant the original ethical relationship. Instead, there is a *never-ending oscillation* between ethics and politics," Simmons is even more explicit about the mutuality of the ethical and political realms when he says, in summary,

> Levinas uses the relationship between philosophy and non-philosophy, Same and Other, ontology and ethics, autonomy and heteronomy, Hellenism and Judaism, and most importantly for the discussion in this chapter, ethics and politics [*sic*—It should read 'politics and ethics']. Each unit of the pair is *mutually interdependent*, but the second unit, although pre-original, has been neglected in the Western philosophical tradition, while the hegemonic first term has been unrestrained. Levinas seeks to *restore balance* to the pairs without ignoring either.

Simmons goes on to say that "Levinas's philosophy begins and ends with politics."[39] This sort of 'mutual interdependence' or 'balance' that has Levinas's philosophy beginning and ending with politics is surely inaccurate, however, since Levinas explicitly says just the opposite. Levinas says that politics does not have the first word or the last word. Politics, as concern for the ego, "is neither first nor last" (OB, 128).[40] By giving this interpretation, Simmons is able, like Ferreira, to rescue Levinas from the charge of incoherence and the charge that he rejects all theories of justice. The cost of such an interpretation, however, is that it is unable to account for true asymmetry that is so central to Levinas's project. One would have to accept the explanation that Levinas was attempting to do *nothing more* than to balance out the priority that politics currently enjoys.

We have covered three types of interpretation now—two types which suggested a mere reversal of priority, and one that suggested a mere mutuality of priority. The first two types tried to stay true to the asymmetry of the ethical relation at the expense of denying mutuality, while the mutuality option allows for mutuality only at the cost of neutering Levinas's asymmetry. Do any other options remain open to us? I will now turn to a fourth option that bears resemblance to the mutuality interpretation, but which does so without dismissing the asymmetry.

§5 Pacific Inversion of Priority

A fourth interpretation is what I will call the 'pacific inversion of priority'[41] or 'pacific priority.' Levinas uses the term himself, saying that the relation with the Other is "fundamentally pacific" (TI, 171).[42] Pacific priority is a priority of hierarchy, but it has Levinas inverting the priority of ontology and the ethical relation without making the change in priority a mere reversal of priority. Pacific priority also rejects the view that the change in priority is accomplished through mutuality, because it admits the persistence of the hierarchy of the Other over myself. Unlike the mutuality view, there is a hierarchy, but unlike the reversal views, the hierarchy is qualitatively different from the priority that has ontology dominating the ethical relation.

One who also endorses this view, or something like it, is Peter Atterton. Although he doubts whether it is possible, Atterton writes, "The violence corresponding to the necessity of the logos (speech, universality, ontology and so on) . . . [is] neither chronologically nor logically posterior to the non-violence of ethics." He rejects a chronological or logical priority, but like the mutuality interpretations, he shows how the origin of language in the third prevents the Derridean reading of a mere priority reversal. One reason he rejects this reversal interpretation is that it would force one to say that advocating such a reversal is tantamount to suggesting a mutual priority (which Levinas clearly rejects). Ignoring the role of the third—as Derrida does— would require one to say that "neither peace nor violence . . . could call itself primordial (only equiprimordial)."[43] Atterton rejects this equiprimordiality because it flatly contradicts Levinas's insistence that "The face to face remains an ultimate situation" (TI, 81).

One must ask, therefore, why those like Ferreira and Simmons, having recognized the role of the third in the origin of language, turn to the option of mutuality. If one thinks that the only options are 1) priority of ontology over ethics; 2) a reversal of (1); or 3) mutual priority between ontology and ethics, then (3) is the only choice left once (1) is eliminated because Levinas rejected it, and (2) is rejected because of the rejection of a mere reversal. Option (3) is also desirable for the reason that it is one with which we are familiar. Perhaps Ferreira and Simmons saw option (3) as the best alternative, given the fact that they knew Levinas denied both of the first two options. The fact is, however, that Levinas rejects this simple mutuality as well, and the most faithful way to interpret Levinas is to reject all three of the above options. This priority 'pacific inversion' interpretation passes the Gyges test on all accounts because it rejects Gyges' unseen seer, it rejects the reverse of Gyges (the unseeing seen), but it also maintains the asymmetrical priority of the Other who is the one who "breaks Gyges' secret."

The question is whether this pacific interpretation is a plausible or even a possible position. Even Atterton, who defends this interpretive option, reveals his doubts about its possibility. "Any such founding [of language upon the ethical relation] *should it exist*, confounds any straightforward logical or chronological ordering of terms or events."[44] The caveat, 'should it exist' shows that he is doubtful about whether it actually exists. No wonder then, that some turn to mutuality, because the 'pacific priority' interpretation has two strikes against it. First, it is difficult to find a definition that is not a purely negative description (i.e., it is not a straightforward reversal, and it is *not* an equiprimordial mutuality). Second, it is difficult to find champions of such a priority who also find it plausible. Thus, it will be my task to suggest an account of this pacific priority that shows it to be possible and plausible and to do so in terms that are not just negative.

Authority and Power

In order to see this how pacific inversion of hierarchical priority is plausible, it is imperative to notice the distinction Levinas makes between 'authority' and 'power.'[45] It is a distinction which I have not seen emphasized in the secondary literature, but it is one on which I think the very plausibility of his project hangs.

The problem as I presented it earlier is that Levinas clearly shows that the ethical relation has authority over ontology and likewise, the Other has authority over me. It seems at first glance that Ricoeur's depiction and criticism of Levinas's face of the Other as a "master of justice" that forcefully "forbids murder"[46] might be accurate. Levinas denounces domination, but in endorsing the domination of the ego by the Other, it looks as if he is contradicting himself. Challenging Levinas on this apparent contradiction, an interviewer posed the following question: "The face commands that one welcome it. Now, if the commandment is absolute, how can people act unethically? Does a violent action indicate that the person has not recognized the commandment? Or is it possible to recognize an absolute commandment as such and to disobey it in spite of this recognition?" (PM, 175).

"Certainly," he replied. "The face is not a force. It is an *authority*. Authority is often without force" (PM, 175). Elsewhere in the interview he said that the Other, who calls me to infinite responsibility, "is not a force but an authority" (PM, 169). This is not just a distinction he makes late in his life. We can find the same distinction throughout the corpus. For example, he made the same distinction, though less explicitly, when he wrote that the alterity of the Other is "manifested in a mastery that does not conquer" (TI, 171). Thus Ricoeur's depiction of the face as a forceful master of justice misses the mark, since although the face of the Other has authority, it does not necessarily have the power to enforce it.[47] Despite the fact that the Other speaks to me from on high, the "Relation with the Other . . . is *fundamentally pacific*" (TI, 171). We can also see this distinction made when Levinas speaks of the authority of the Other which "does not do violence to the I" (TI, 47).

That authority and power are separable can be seen elsewhere in the corpus as well. We find Levinas speaking of "a double expression of weakness and strict, urgent requirement" (PJL, 108). The strict, urgent requirement is the transcendent authority, but that this comes to us without enforcement is seen by the fact that it is also 'weak'—that is, without power. Again, in yet another essay, Levinas affirms the compatibility of "two apparently contradictory things: the appearance of weakness . . . [and] an authority in the face." This apparent paradox is emphasized yet again when we find that in "the face which is the most naked and exposed state of human existence . . . there is also the command."[48]

That should be sufficient textual support for the fact that this distinction exists between authority and power, and that often authority is without power. If one fails to see this distinction, then the 'pacific inversion of priority' that Levinas suggests will seem utterly implausible. If authority is thought to be identical to power, then the only options to the hierarchical rule of ontology are to exchange one power for another, the elimination of authority altogether, or to have a mutual sharing of power. No other option exists if authority and power are coextensive.

If, however, authority is separable from power, then another option emerges. Not only is it possible for there to be power without authority (which is injustice), but there can be authority without power (which is the ethical relation). If authority and power are separable, then what is the nature of this authority that is without power? In what way does this constitute a pacific relation, and how, if at all, is this authority good?

Is the Authority Good?

How is it that this pacific relation is truly different from a violent hierarchy? Levinas calls "ontology . . . as first philosophy" a "philosophy of power" (TI, 46), but "ethics as first philosophy" is never dubbed first in power. The inverse that Levinas calls for is one that is quite different. He wrote that ontology (the comprehension of Being) "*cannot dominate* the relationship with the Other. The latter relationship *commands* the first" (TI, 47). Here it looks as if this might be the mere reversal discussed earlier—a reversal of command. But the inversion is pacific since it is a change from 'demand' (of power) to a 'command' (of authority). To demand is to force, whereas to command is to speak from authority. The command, unlike the demand, does not necessarily have power, and the demand, unlike the command, does not necessarily have authority. The relation is maintained "without violence, in peace with this absolute alterity" (TI, 197). Furthermore, "the 'resistance' of the other does not do violence to me, does not act negatively; it has a positive structure: ethical" (TI, 197). But these texts are from *Totality and Infinity*. Does this pacific priority persist into his later work?

Indeed, in *Otherwise than Being*, we find that this authority is not only called 'the Good' but that "no one is enslaved to the Good" (11). Furthermore, despite the asymmetry of my being "for the Other," it is nonetheless "without alienation" (OB, 114). If that is not sufficiently convincing, we find again that this "authority . . . [involves] a turning away from the use of force" (DR, 175). We can conclude, then, that this pacific relation is ultimately a relation with the Good, and it does not leave me alienated, enslaved, or the unwilling victim of violence.

This leads us to another important qualification. It is an authority without violence in the sense that the violence can be refused, but that does not mean that this peacefulness guarantees me an absence of suffering. If suffering or violence is willingly accepted—that is, if the authority is obeyed and this brings me into suffering, what can be said about that violence?

Is Violence Redeemed?

I raised this question already in chapter 3 when I asked whether Levinas was willing to "preach sacrifice" that is without promise of reward. I suggested there that even though he does not promise reward, it is quite possible that he thinks that virtue is its own reward. I suggested that he may have hope in the promise but be unwilling to promise the promise to others for fear of how that might manipulate others to make sacrifices for him.

But in the context of suffering violence in obedience to authority or the Good, we can find even more reason to think that Levinas was hopeful for the value of that violence. At one point, Levinas says that my "responsibility for another is . . . imposed with a good violence" (OB, 43). What is meant by good, though? This is stated more clearly when he says that 'substitution' or 'being for the Other' is not initiated by the one who is substituting, but this is chosen by the Good.[49] "But being Good *it redeems the violence* of its alterity, even if the subject has to suffer through the augmentation of this ever more demanding violence" (OB, 15; my emphasis). That sounds quite hopeful, as it does later when he writes that in this trauma of being for the Other, "the Good reabsorbs, or redeems, the violence of non-freedom" (OB, 123). So the authority is not only separable from force, but obedience to the suffering required by the authority is redeemed by the Good.

Does Authority Make a Difference?

The fact that authority and power can be separate suggests that they can be opposed to each other—one can use power to oppose authority, and this may even serve as a definition of injustice. But the possibility of power contradicting authority does not entail that authority and power are always opposed to each other. In fact authority with power may be one way of characterizing justice. And as we saw earlier, the introduction of the third requires justice and judgments and wisdom, therefore it requires that some degree of power accompany authority. But if the introduction of the third introduces the necessity of justice (authority that uses power), and there is always a third, then it looks as if we will never have authority that is completely without power. How then is the justice that Levinas recommends any different from the justice he critiques? The question, simply put, is this: "So what?" Even if it is possible for the ethical relation to have this pacific priority over ontology, and even if it is possible for love to have this pacific priority over wisdom, what practical difference does it make? If we get a democratically organized state on Levinas's account just as we do on Hobbes's account of the origin of the state, what is the difference?

Levinas responds to this sort of question saying that "[i]t is not unimportant to know . . . whether the egalitarian and just State in which the European realizes himself . . . proceeds from a war of all against all—or from the irreducible responsibility of one for the other, and whether it can ignore the uniqueness of the face and of love" (PP, 144). It is with that question in mind that I now turn to the next chapter. Levinas thinks it is a distinction with a difference, so let us examine that difference.

This chapter has focused on what Levinas meant by 'service' in the phrase, "philosophy is the wisdom of love at the *service* of love," and has shown that 'service' or 'priority,' as Levinas uses it, is not a reversal of priority or a mutualization of priority but rather, is a pacific inversion of priority. I have also indicated how such a pacific priority is possible once we see the distinction between authority and power. It is the task of chapter 5 to explore what Levinas meant by wisdom. That is, what might a wisdom of love look like if it were in service to love, and how, if at all, is it any different from wisdom not so conceived?

Chapter 5

Levinasian Wisdom

La philosophie: *sagesse* de l'amour au service de l'amour

As we continue this examination of Levinas's central phrase that philosophy is "the wisdom of love at the service of love," the groundwork has been laid to now turn to an analysis of Levinas's 'wisdom of love.' Chapter 2 outlined many terms used by Levinas that are closely related with wisdom of love, including 'philosophy,' 'judgment,' 'comparison,' 'calculation,' 'measure,' 'quantification,' 'language,' 'speech,' 'thought,' 'knowledge,' 'science,' 'thematization,' 'intelligence,' 'Said,' 'intentionality,' 'ontology,' 'comprehension of being,' 'objectivity,' 'representation,' 'justice,' 'state,' 'politics,' 'institutions,' 'legislation,' and 'law.' We can draw from all these different, yet linked, terms to help us come to a clearer understanding of 'wisdom of love.' In chapter 3, we saw what sort of love it is that wisdom of love serves and in chapter 4, we saw the way in which this priority relationship is a pacific hierarchy of love over wisdom— a hierarchy of authority, not one of power. Throughout all of these chapters, I have been arguing *against* the interpretation that has Levinas suggesting we embrace a wisdom without wisdom or a politics without politics or thematization without thematizing. Such views are understandably criticized as being performatively self-contradictory, and while some of Levinas's contemporaries and interpreters may embrace such contradictions and revel in the very impossibility of it all, I have argued that Levinas does not take such a position.

I discussed in chapter 4 how wisdom arises once the third is introduced, and since "there is always a third" (PJL, 104), wisdom is necessary—there must always be a comparison between the Other and the third, since one cannot fulfill infinite responsibility to more than one. The necessity of wisdom is explicit throughout the corpus, such as when Levinas says that "[j]ustice is necessary, that is, comparison, coexistence, contemporaneousness, assembling, order, thematizations" (OB, 157). It is especially made clear in the later essays, such as when he speaks of the "necessity for a 'weighing,' a comparison, a pondering" (PJL, 104), and elsewhere when he says that the "relation with the other and the unique, which is peace, comes to require a reason that thematizes and synchronizes and synthesizes, that thinks the world and reflects on being; concepts necessary to the peace of men" (PP, 142). This thinking is a 'necessity,' it is 'required,' and not merely a necessity that must be tolerated as a necessary evil, but as that which is required for peace.

Hopefully, it is now clear enough that Levinas recognizes the necessity of wisdom, and that the wisdom of love, which he advocates, is not some ideal that is historically and actually impossible, but is something that is coherent and possible in this world. The objection that surely arises in response to this conclusion, however, is that if wisdom is necessary, and we must have thematizing, comparisons, judgment, speech, politics, and the whole lot, then this prophetic message of Levinas does not sound so prophetic after all. Indeed, how is what Levinas suggests any different from wisdom, justice, and politics as usual? If the authority of the ethical relation and the absence of thematizing only occurs when there is just the Other and I, and this never occurs (since there is always a third), then is Levinas's point merely hypothetical and academic? What is the difference between a wisdom of love and a love of wisdom in this world where I, in fact, find many third parties? The primary task of this chapter is to answer that objection by showing that there is a difference—a significant difference—not only in theory, but in practice.

§1 Wisdom of Love: Origins

Theoretically, a central feature of wisdom of love is the fact that it originates not in a war of all against all, as Hobbes would have it, but in the absolute responsibility of one for the Other. Throughout the corpus, Levinas inveighs against the social contract view of political association, such as when he states that politics is not "harmonizing antagonistic forces" (OB, 159). Love of wisdom differs from wisdom of love in that the former views politics as originating in original war. "The order of politics," says Levinas, "which inaugurates the 'social contract' is neither the sufficient condition nor the necessary outcome of ethics. In its ethical position, the self is distinct from the citizen born of the City, and from the individual who precedes all order in his natural egoism, from whom political philosophy, since Hobbes, tries to derive—or succeeds in deriving—the social or political order of the city" (US, 165).

The way that institutions, politics, justice, speech, and wisdom trace their origin to the responsibility for the Other is addressed across a broad range of Levinas's texts, but is most clearly and succinctly explained in "Peace and Proximity."[1] In this essay, Levinas describes how the original relation is that between the I and the Other; this relationship is one of "responsibility for the other" and it is "prior to all questions" (PP, 142). To raise a question at the time when I am alone with the Other would be violent to the Other, because it would be to question my responsibility for the Other and to seek to put a limit on my limitless responsibility for the Other. But when the third comes along, this is the "birth of the question" because now I must ask "What am I to do?" and "Which one comes before the other in my responsibility?" (PP, 142). This question then requires comparison, because I must compare two incomparables in order to discern which one I am to serve first. In making these comparisons, I must thematize or generalize about them so that they can be compared. If this were done without the presence of the third requiring it, then this thematizing would be reducing the irreducible Other to a theme, but now that this comparison is required to answer the question, thematizing becomes a necessity for the purpose of loving the Other and the third. This thematizing requires thought and gives rise to "the necessity of thinking together beneath one synthetic theme the multiple and the unity of the world" (PP, 143). From this thinking comes political structure. And of course, political structure requires law to govern the structure and institutions to carry out the law. This last progression from thought to politics to law to institutions is summed when Levinas writes: "finally thereby [by thought] the extreme importance in human multiplicity of the political structure of society under the rule of law, and hence institutions in which the *for-the-other* [of the I] . . . enters with the dignity of the citizen in the perfect reciprocity of political laws that are essentially egalitarian or held to become so" (PP, 143; my emphasis).

In an even more concise summary, we could say that the origin of the political state and its institutions begins with the ethical relation between I and the Other, and then the presence of the third gives rise to the birth of the question which requires comparison which requires thought which gives rise to political laws which give rise to political structure. This genealogy of politics is in sharp contrast to the genealogy of the state offered by Hobbes, according to which the state originates with the I who is for himself and thus compares, thinks and makes judgments for the sake of self-preservation and decides it is best for his own preservation to make a contractual truce with the Other whereby there is a mutual prohibition of killing.

One might observe that both the Levinasian and Hobbesian genealogies of political wisdom could allow for an egalitarian democracy. If that is the case, then a pressing question in response to this analysis of the origin of the state, politics, and wisdom is this: What *practical difference* does it make whether the democratic state has a pedigree as Hobbes describes or as Levinas describes? If both accounts yield the same political state, then why bother understanding the source?

§2 Wisdom and Authority

As seen in the last chapter, wisdom of love is wisdom that is in service to love, and this service indicates that love of the Other (the ethical relation) has a pacific hierarchical authority over me. We saw that this pacific priority depended upon a distinction between authority and force and a particular understanding of that authority. How then do authority and force, so understood, have any bearing on this discussion of wisdom?

In short, we can observe that the wisdom of love is a wisdom that is in service to love—to that authority, and all the comparisons and judgments that are made with a wisdom of love are made with respect to this authority. The way we saw that this hierarchical priority avoids becoming tyrannical is by noticing that the authority of the Other does not entail the power of the Other. In fact the authority may be powerless. Levinas points to the apparently contradictory combination of authority and powerlessness saying, "There is, in the face, the supreme authority that commands," but the face of the Other has an apparently "contradictory nature. It is all weakness and all authority" (PO, 105). Understanding the uniqueness of wisdom of love depends largely on understanding how it is possible for the Other to have authority over me without having power over me.

When Levinas speaks of the Other having authority over me that is 'absolute' (PL, 175), or 'infinite' (DR, 175), it is not absolute or infinite in the sense that it cannot be disobeyed since the "infinite and indeclinable authority . . . does not prevent disobedience" (DR, 175). The absolute nature of the authority of the Other lies in the fact that the authority does not wax or wane with my compliance or rebellion. It is authority that is not lessened by my disobedience. How, then, does this commanding, nondemanding authority help us understand wisdom of love? It helps us by providing the framework that marks the primary difference between a wisdom of love and a love of wisdom—a framework wherein it is possible that wisdom of love yields to the command of the authority without demand. Wisdom of love is a wisdom that acknowledges this authority and makes comparisons, measurements, thematizations, and judgments that recognize this authority. This acknowledgment of the authority is something that is awakened. Wisdom of love is 'thought' that breaks through the "impassive soul of pure knowledge" and causes "an awakening to the other man in his uniqueness" (PP, 139). Wisdom of love is wisdom that is alert to the authority of the Other which has always existed, even before I became aware of it.

This hierarchical authority of the love of the Other holds true not just for the individual, but for philosophies, systems of justice, and political institutions. It is "very important . . . that justice should flow from, issue from the preeminence of the other. The institutions that justice requires must be subject to the oversight of the charity from which justice issued" (VF, 176). But it is important to point out the obvious fact that this wisdom of love (whether individual or political) is not the equivalent of the authority to which it is subject. The wisdom, unlike the authority to which it is subject, is always fallible, and even though the authority of love is absolute, the wisdom (even the wisdom subject to the authority of love) always "risks preventing the face of the other man from being recognized" (VF, 176).

To better understand this wisdom of love in service to an absolute authority that "does not prevent disobedience" (DR, 176), I will turn to the following question: how is it that this authority can be disobeyed, and what good can such a powerless authority hope to accomplish?

§3 Authority Obeyed and Disobeyed

The absolute authority under examination is the authority of the Other whose face says, "thou shall commit murder" (TI, 262). That this authority, if it exists, can be disobeyed can be shown empirically, and the empirical evidence is ample. So before turning to disobedience, perhaps it is best to look first at this authority and why it is said to be absolute. Since our evidence for disobedience will be empirical, I will begin by pointing to empirical evidence in favor of this authority.[2] The examples from which I will draw[3] empirical evidence all concern the choice between participating in the murder of another and risking one's own well-being. They are examples of life-and-death situations. It may be objected that such examples are extreme and that they do not have much bearing on the ordinary ethical decisions that ordinary humans must face every day. I have three responses to such an objection.

First, the choices people make in life-and-death situations are not as extraordinary as it may seem. Those who chose to kill seem extraordinarily demonic or insane while those who chose to risk their own lives rather than kill seem extraordinarily heroic. But what we shall see is that both were done by ordinary people, and are described by those making the decisions as being very ordinary indeed. Secondly, I wish to point out that Levinas was highly concerned with what one does in these life-and-death situations. His most common description of what the face of the Other commands is "thou shall not kill." And Levinas dedicated *Otherwise than Being* to "the memory of those who were closest among the six million assassinated by the National Socialists" (v), and those events clearly played a major role in his writing. So we would not be surprised to discover that it was important for Levinas to discover an ethic that allowed one to pass the test of these life-and-death situations. Third, the focus of this chapter is to show how it is that wisdom of love differs from other types of wisdom, and it is precisely in such situations of life and death where the difference is most clearly seen. As the twentieth century has borne out, such events are not as uncommon or abnormal as we would like them to be, and there is not a quarter of the globe or a quarter of that century that is unfamiliar with mass murder where such life-and-death choices had to be made. It is perhaps appropriate that I draw my examples from the genocide that most affected Levinas himself—the Jewish Holocaust.

Attending to the Authority of the Other

The first set of examples[4] comes from a small village, Le Chambon, in southern France. In that village, during the German occupation of France during the Second World War, a woman by the name of Magda Trocmé was faced with a face. She describes the encounter saying that a "German woman knocked on my door. It was in the evening, and she said she was a German Jew, coming from northern France, that she was in danger, and that she had heard that in Le Chambon somebody could help her. Could she come into my house? I said, 'Naturally, come in, and come in.' Lots of snow. She had a little pair of shoes, nothing." In this encounter she had a simple choice to help this person and risk her own life and the lives of those in her village (since harboring Jews was forbidden). But to send her away, when she knew no one else would harbor her, would have been to have done harm since from the point of view of the refugee, "turning somebody away from one's door is not simply a refusal to help; it is an *act of harmdoing.*"[5]

This entire community eventually became a safe haven for endangered Jews throughout the last four and most dangerous years of the German occupation. Yet, no type of reasoning could convince them to stop taking these risks for the sake of other humans. The people of Le Chambon "would not give up a life for any price—for their own comfort, for their own safety, for patriotism, or for legality." Nothing could trump the limitless value of a human life, and as Philip Hallie comments, "[f]or those who believe in the absolute preciousness of life, there is no proof that the feelings and images involved in such a belief are correct or even plausible." The experience of Magda Trocmé and the others in Le Chambon gives testimony to the fact that the life of the individual Other who shows up at one's door in need of life-giving help has an absolute authority. It is not something that can be proven, but that which is properly basic cannot be proven by means of something else—it simply is a brute fact, and other conclusions are reached as a result of this properly basic fact. The authority of the Other is such an absolute authority, and the testimony of the villagers in Le Chambon attests to this.

When people of Le Chambon were interviewed years later and asked why they risked their lives for the chance of helping a stranger, they would answer like Madame Eyraud who "could never fully understand what [Hallie] was getting at" in asking that question. She simply said, "Look. Look. Who else would have taken care of them if we didn't? They needed our help, and they needed it *then*." It was that simple. No further explanation was needed. No one requested proof that the human life must not be forfeited. Others would answer the question with a shrug. "Well, where else could they go? I had to take them in." They were not standing on an elevated moral ground; they did not describe their actions as supererogatory. After interviewing many of them, reading their accounts, and spending much time with them, Hallie described their actions as an "undivided attention to the lucid mystery of being alive for others and for ourselves."[6] That is a wisdom of love—attention to the mystery of being alive for the Other. But of course, it is possible to turn our attention away from this mystery. That is why this absolute authority can be disobeyed. Examples of disobedience of this authority, of course, are not difficult to find—especially during the same time period that the Chambonnais were obeying that authority by illegally harboring Jews.

Ignoring the Authority of the Other

Robert Lifton, in his important work interviewing dozens of Nazi doctors, assesses how they were able to violate their oaths to do no harm and to go so far as to contribute to the murder of thousands of Jews in the concentration camp at Auschwitz. If such an absolute authority exists, as Levinas claims and as the Chambonnais gave testimony, then how could such an absolute authority be so absolutely disobeyed? Lifton confirmed Hannah Arendt's[7] assessment of these atrocities—namely that great evil can be done by ordinary people. It was difficult for Lifton and others to face "the disturbing psychological truth that participation in mass murder need not require emotions as extreme or demonic as would seem appropriate for such a malignant project." These doctors, who were trained to heal and sustain life, were able to maintain fairly ordinary lives of spending time with their families, going on holidays, enjoying cultivated conversations. Like many criminal subcultures such as the Mafia, a person can on the one hand order or carry out a cold-blooded murder "while remaining a loving husband, father, and churchgoer."[8]

If the authority of the face that commands "thou shall not kill me" is indeed absolute, and not relative or constructed in some way, then it seems strange that such a seemingly ordinary life could be sustained in the midst of such an extraordinary violation of that authority. So how can this be done? Levinas argues that such violations are due to the fact that the authority does not necessarily force compliance and that this authority can be overpowered by being ignored. It is ignored in various ways, and it can be done by what Levinas calls becoming 'invisible' to the Other. I will argue that the authority of the Other can be disobeyed by ignoring the authority of the Other, and that it is ignored by becoming invisible to the Other. Likewise, when the Other is truly visible to me, obedience to that authority is only natural and normal. This invisibility explains the ordinariness of the seemingly extraordinary Nazi evil just as the visibility explains the ordinariness of the seemingly extraordinary heroic acts of the Chambonnais. Of course, this is not to say that there is no significant difference—of course there is an enormous difference between the two ways of responding to the refugee, but the point revealed by invisibility is that the normal response is to invite the refugee in, and that the very different and heinous response of killing the refugee is carried out by making it appear normal to those who do it. It is made to appear normal through this process of becoming invisible to the face of the Other.

But what is meant by this invisibility which empowers one to ignore the absolute authority of the Other and the visibility which leads to following that authority? That is the question to which I now turn.

§4 Becoming Invisible

As we saw in chapter 4, the person who has wisdom of love is not invisible but is visible to the Other, and this very visibility is in fact a central defining feature of the wisdom of love. Although Levinas does not explore in explicitly practical terms how this invisibility applies to ethical encounters with the Other, I will do so here as a part of making the case that a wisdom of love is different from other types of wisdom. The invisibility that wisdom of love seeks to avoid is not just metaphorical—it can mean literal invisibility, such that one avoids being called into question by the face of the Other by physically guarding oneself from the gaze of that face. But it also can mean a conceptual invisibility. We saw in chapter 4 that visibility did not refer only to physical sight, but also had connotations of cognition, such that to see the Other is to conceptualize the Other, just as to be seen by the Other is to be conceptualized by the Other.

Invisibility could be attained ideologically by reducing the Other to a mere instance of a category, thereby eliminating her unique human face. By making the Other a token of a type, and separating myself ideologically from that type, I can make myself invisible to the face of that Other once I have reduced her. Invisibility by cognition can also be psychological such that one views oneself differently in order to deceive oneself into thinking that I am not responsible for the Other. In each case, though, the invisibility makes it possible to disobey the authority of the Other without having to oppose it directly. Invisibility gives one power to disobey that authority by distancing oneself from direct awareness of that authority. Even if the thought process does not consciously follow this pattern, the result is that one need not live with the constant difficulty of knowing that one is disobeying absolute authority, when he can simply become invisible to its gaze and continue his ordinary life relatively undisturbed. Various ways of becoming invisible enable a disobedience of the absolute authority.

Of course, this invisibility has implications for responsibility, since to be seen by the Other is to be called into question by the face of the Other. To be called into question by the face of the Other is to be responsible for the Other. Thus, becoming invisible is a way I can deceive myself into thinking that I am not responsible for the Other.

But in order to help answer the question of how wisdom of love is practically different from other types of wisdom, I will now address more specifically how this secret invisibility actually occurs. Seeing the ways that we become invisible to others will help demonstrate that some types of wisdom encourage invisibility, and that others encourage visibility and thus responsibility for the Other.

Drawing from Lifton's analysis of the Nazi doctors, we can see all three types of invisibility at work—physical, ideological, and psychological. Levinas speaks of encountering the authority of the Other in the empirical encounter of that particular Other, and although he also speaks of conceptual invisibility to the Other, it is easy to overlook the fact that this authority and its avoidance, as well, can be quite concretely *physical*. The physical invisibility plays a major role in hiding from the authority that is found in that face.

For example, the evolving of the methodology for Nazi killing gives evidence to the difficulty of physically looking victims in the face. The earliest method used in the killing of Jews was execution by gun, but the Nazis involved in this (the *Einsatzgruppen*) experienced difficulties in this "face-to-face killing." One of the *Einsatzgruppen* generals, after watching the execution of about a hundred Jews, observed those who had been doing the face-to-face killing and declared, "Look at the eyes of [these men,] how deeply shaken they are! These men are finished for the rest of their lives."[9] To look these victims in the face and kill them caused the killers to have physical ailments as well as psychic exhaustion and hallucinations. Disobeying the authority of the face of the Other had great tolls on those who did so, and this became apparent early on. The ideological reduction of the Other may have succeeded in allowing the *Einsatzgruppen* to be able to kill, but the physical visibility of the face worked strongly to undermine the ideological invisibility.

The fact that face-to-face killing was so difficult led Heinrich Himmler to develop methods—which included the gas chambers—that helped make the killers virtually unseen (physically) by the victims, thus making the task much easier. "The shift from face-to-face killing by the *Einsatzgruppen* to the elaborate machinery of the gas chambers can be said to have diminished the degree of the ordeal" even though the ordeal of it was never removed completely. The task of killing was first of all divided into several discrete tasks performed by different people, so that no one person had to see the victim all the way through the process. The doctors who were involved in making 'selections' of those who would be sent to the gas chambers did not themselves put the victims in the chambers, turn on the gas, or have to remove the dead bodies. "It could largely succeed," as one Nazi doctor later recalled, "because dead bodies *did not have to be viewed*." Even those assistants who had the most direct contact with the victims did not have to watch during the gassing, but "could look through the peephole to confirm that people inside the gas chamber were dead."[10]

The use of the Zyklon-B gas, as opposed to bullets, meant that those involved "no longer had to experience the horrors of face-to-face killing. As one Nazi later admitted in testimony, 'I always shuddered at the prospects of carrying out exterminations by shooting.' "[11] The problems that were experienced by having to physically look at the faces of the victims give evidence to the fact that one, indeed, encounters an authority in the face of the Other that commands them not to kill.[12] It helps to explain why invisibility is so crucial in allowing one to disobey that authority.

Physical invisibility, though important, was not the only method of becoming invisible to the victim. As seen above, even with all of the routines, the separation of tasks, and the visual shielding, participation in the process was still "an ordeal." Behind it all, therefore, was the necessity of an invisibility enabled by ideology—that is, a commitment to an ideal that helped hide the uniqueness of the Other behind a veil of ideology. In this case, it is obvious that the Nazi political ideology was crucial in allowing the Nazis to see the Jews as less than the unique humans that they were.

Also playing a key role was the biomedical ideology—seeing the Nazi state as a 'biocracy' wherein "the divine prerogative was that of cure through purification and revitalization of the Aryan race." At work in the minds of most of these doctors was a participation in an ideologically grand vision of biological purification that was supported by rationality and science. "Highly important to the German-Nazi ethos was the claim to logic, rationality, and science." One doctor when being interviewed became irate at the mention that the concentration camp attitudes were possibly similar to those in the Jonestown suicide-murder, since the latter was a form of idealism and stupidity whereas his Auschwitz had "carefully considered questions of logic and theory." For scientific verification of their ideological program, they appealed to such theories as logical positivism and Darwinism.[13] These appeals to logic, science, and rationality served to make the perpetrators invisible to the authority of the individuals they were murdering, because between themselves and the faces of those individuals, they were placing a conceptual veil that distorted those particular human faces in a way that obscured the authority therein.

Many of these conceptual veils made their violations of the authority of the Other appear to the perpetrator as an act contributing to the greater good. This sometimes took the simple form of using euphemistic terminology to hide the authority of the Other. The Nazis would speak of their killing as 'evacuations,' 'disinfection,' or 'delousing.' Sometimes it was even called 'natural selection,' which simultaneously gave it an acceptable term and gave the action an appearance of scientific legitimacy. These terms accompanied the conceptual masks placed on the Other—masks that made the Other appear to them as 'vermin' which needed to be 'exterminated' or as a 'disease' or the 'germ of death' which needed to be 'removed' in order to 'heal'[14] the human race.

While the physical and ideological invisibility played an important role in allowing the Nazis to ignore the authority of the Other, present in nearly every Nazi doctor Lifton interviewed was evidence of *psychological* invisibility. The most common and effective technique of invisibility that Lifton discovered in the Nazi doctors he interviewed was the psychological technique of what he called 'doubling.' The Nazi doctors spoke of what they did in the camps in third person, describing their actions as if describing the actions of someone else. Lifton found that they each had created an autonomous 'Auschwitz self' that was psychologically in charge of the actions involved in the killing. All the while, there remained a psychologically autonomous self with which the doctor would identify. This 'Auschwitz self' did the dirty work and also, therefore, received the blame, while the Nazi doctor would identify with a different self who spent time with his family and socialized with friends. In this way, they avoided guilt "not by the elimination of conscience but by what can be called the *transfer of conscience*."[15] This supports the conclusion that the authority of the Other is difficult to flatly and directly overpower. Instead, the self creates a second self, which is the one that looks on the Other for the self. It is in this way that one can become psychologically invisible to the Other, and thus hide from the accusation of the Other's face.

Psychological methods of invisibility also could include self-serving distortion of the Other along with persistent forgetting—all ways of disassociating oneself with the face of the Other. Also described by all of the doctors was a sense of hopelessness. If one thinks there is nothing one can do to avoid the violence they are about to commit, then it helps one ignore the authority of the Other. If I think I am powerless to obey the command of the Other, then it makes me feel free to avoid acting on the Other's behalf. One Nazi doctor explained his actions by recalling thinking at the time, "Well what can be done? First of all we are powerless, we can't change this situation."[16] The obvious irony is that claiming to be powerless to help the Other actually serves to give one power over the Other—being powerless gives one power over the authority of the Other and contributes to the ease with which one becomes invisible to the Other. The psychological effect of hopelessness is just one important implication for the hopefulness of Levinas's wisdom of love. The fact that Levinas thinks wisdom of love is possible and not merely some abstract impossible ideal helps remove this psychological method of becoming invisible.

Thus, we can see that there was an overlapping of methods—physical, ideological, and psychological—which all contribute to one's becoming invisible to the accusing face of the Other. In the example of the Nazi doctors, we find that whatever method or combination of methods was employed, the doctors were able to distance themselves from the victims and thereby reject responsibility for their deaths. "Whether a Nazi doctor saw Jews without feeling their presence, or *did not see them* at all, he no longer experienced them as beings who affected him."[17]

§5 Becoming Visible

In order to continue answering the question of how this wisdom of love is different not only in theory, but also in practice, it will be helpful for us to ask this question of our examples. Just as we viewed some actual examples of invisibility (in Auschwitz) and asked how these exemplified the process of becoming invisible, so it can be helpful to look at examples of visibility (in Le Chambon) in order to see what might be revealed about how one becomes visible.

So what was it about the villagers in Le Chambon that might have helped them remain visible to those who sought their help? If others during the same time period could become sufficiently invisible to the Jews to kill them, then certainly they could have become invisible enough to at least send the refugees elsewhere. But they did not. Why? Just as the Nazis became physically, ideologically, and psychologically invisible, so the Chambonnais exemplified physical, ideological, and psychological visibility.

Whereas the Nazi concentration camps were designed in such a way to visually shield the killers from the victims, the Chambonnais opened their doors to the Jewish refugees and continued to keep them in their field of vision, inviting the refugees into their homes. There were no steps taken to remove the Jews from their sight, except in order to hide them.

Beliefs also played a key role in helping the Chambonnais become and remain visible to the refugees. Hallie is convinced that in much the same way ideological beliefs played a major role in making the Nazi doctors invisible to their victims, the beliefs of the Chambonnais were central in motivating and giving strength to the conviction that they should risk their lives in order to provide hiding for the many Jews who came to their doorsteps. Although Hallie is unable to say for sure whether he believed the survival of these many Jews was a miracle, he is quite clear that the beliefs of the villagers were essential to the effort. After studying the event and interviewing many involved, Hallie says that the "leader of the rescue efforts of the village was the Protestant Pastor Andre Trocmé, who was a passionately religious person. I could not say with confidence that I believed God had worked that miracle through Trocmé, but I had to say in all certainty that Trocmé's belief in God was at the living center of the rescue efforts over four long years." Even if the only evidence is the pragmatic evidence, Hallie nonetheless concludes that "[b]elief in God certainly motivated Trocmé and the villagers, and the love the villagers displayed was indeed effective." Another key leader in the effort, one to whom Trocmé turned for advice on several occasions, was Burns Chalmers, a Quaker. Both Trocmé and Chalmers had a similar commitment to the value of life. The Huguenot (Trocmé) "with three hundred years of French Protestantism behind him and this American (Chalmers) with the international Quaker experience behind him had the same ethical commitment: to treat human life as something beyond all price."[18]

These beliefs, though informed by religion, were not just beliefs to which one gave intellectual assent. Rather, they were deeply personalized and deeply integrated into these people's entire lives. Hallie remarks that the beliefs that allowed the villagers to respond as they did were "personal: they are not to be found by looking around at our public institutions; in the end, they are to be found only in the dreadful solitude of one's own passionate convictions and doubts." The fact that these were not merely intellectual beliefs, but beliefs that were learned by one's very body and bones, is evident in how quickly they respond. These beliefs "are to be found in one's own swift reactions to people and their deeds. They are insubstantial, but they do their work in us: and when they fail, we know, when we do not manage to deceive ourselves, that they have failed to work in us."[19]

Contributing to the visibility of the Chambonnais to the refugees in need was psychological wholeness (in contrast to the Nazi doctors' psychological 'doubling'). In trying to offer an explanation for why Trocmé was so holistic and lacking in the psychological compartmentalization of the Nazis during the same time period, Hallie suggests that Trocmé's "caring came from a lifetime of concern." Trocmé did not have an intellectual self separated from his caring self. Rather, the two affected each other fluidly, such that "his caring was fed by knowledge, and his knowledge was spurred by caring."[20] Just as the Nazi doctors had undergone smaller degrees of doubling before working at the concentration camps, so Hallie suggests that being visible to the Other in a critical situation is learned over a lifetime of being visible to others in smaller situations. The Nazi doctors had learned to become dis-integrated on a smaller scale—they already had begun the process of doubling common among professionals and bureaucrats. For example, doctors usually had to experience doubling by creating a medical self that viewed cadavers, and the Other self, for whom the cadavers were repulsive. Lifton, after interviewing the many Nazi doctors, concluded that to avoid this doubling, we must find ways to become aware of our whole-ness—our integrity.[21] Just as psychological doubling led to invisibility to the authority of the Other, so psychological wholeness led to visibility to the authority of the Other. Trocmé and the Chambonnais exhibited this whole-ness, which resulted in the heroic actions that were described by them as ordinary. To one who is whole, welcoming in a stranger is what they saw as entirely ordinary.

These examples of invisibility and visibility have shown us methods or practices that are employed when one actually becomes invisible or visible to the authority of the Other. But now I want to turn to what Levinas points to as the ultimate source of these methods and practices of becoming invis-ible. We have been spiraling closer and closer to the heart of Levinas's philo-sophical project, and it is now that I think we come as close as we will get to the very center of that heart. What enables this invisibility which enables one to disobey the authority of the Other? This is most clearly seen by looking at the secret of Gyges. I believe that by seeing what the Gyges secret is and how that secret is broken, we come to the center of Levinas's philosophy. So let us turn to that now.

§6 The Secret of Gyges

An examination of Levinas's use of the Gyges myth in chapter 4[22] shows that the Gyges myth was central to Levinas's exposition of the ethical relation because he used Gyges to shed light on invisibility. Gyges is the one who sees without being seen. He is the unseen seer, and there is more to this myth than meets the eye. Levinas speaks of the secret of Gyges (TDT, 104–5), and his desire to break that secret, but before the secret can be broken, we must discover what it is.

Gyges' Secret Question

So what is Gyges' secret? I propose that the answer to that question is a ques-tion, and it is the question of whether it is better to suffer injustice or to inflict it. In this one question lies the secret to Gyges' invisibility,[23] and this can be traced back through the various presentations of Gyges from

Herodotus to Plato to Levinas. I do not have space here to give a full analysis of the various historical, literary, and philosophical uses of Gyges' story, but will give a brief account of a few uses of Gyges in order to suggest that in each case, the question that plays a central role is whether it is better to suffer or inflict injustice.

Herodotus, often referred to as the first historian, begins his first history with the first story of Gyges. In Herodotus's historical account of Gyges,[24] a servant to Phrygian king Kandaules, Gyges is asked by the king to look unseen on the king's wife as she undresses in order to obtain confirmation that his wife is the most beautiful woman Gyges has ever seen. Gyges does not want to do this, but realizes he will lose favor with the king (and thus lose his job, as well) if he does not comply with the king's wishes. The king's wife, however, notices that she has been spied upon, and so she later calls Gyges into her chambers and tells him that for his and the king's offense against her, one of them must die. She tells Gyges that he must either kill her husband, the king, or be killed himself by her guardsmen. This is the Gyges' question in its most obvious form: "Will you kill or be killed?" There apparently was no middle option, so he chose the former option and surreptitiously crept for a second time into the royal chambers to again hide behind a screen before killing the king in his vulnerability. Gyges then married the queen and became the king himself. The physical invisibility of hiding behind the screen was only a secondary invisibility, pointing to the primary invisibility of hiding from the responsibility for the killing of the king. That was Gyges' secret—by appealing to the question of whether it was better to kill or be killed, he convinced himself that he was not responsible for the death of the Other, and convinced others that he was not accountable for the king's death under such circumstances.

In Plato's version of the Gyges story, found in the *Republic*,[25] the mythical account is not very different in essence from Herodotus's historical account, though it does vary in narrative detail. Plato's Gyges uses a ring to make himself invisible, which enables him to kill the king, marry the queen, and set himself up as tyrant. The importance of the myth in Plato's *Republic* becomes clear when the myth is used to bring focus to the question, "is it better to suffer injustice or inflict it?" In other words, if you had the choice to become invisible to the responsibility for your actions, what would you do? Would you choose to suffer injustice over inflicting it, even if you were allowed to inflict it with impunity? Plato, of course, argues that it is better to suffer injustice even if one is able to be invisible to accountability for it.

The Gyges' question (whether it is better to suffer or inflict injustice) is arguably the central question in Greek history's first figure (even if not explicitly so). It is arguably the central question (explicitly and implicitly) of Plato's most famous work. I contend that the question plays a central role in the philosophy of Levinas, as well, or even more so. Levinas says that his entire philosophy can be summed by saying that "there is something more important than my life, and that is the life of the other" (PM, 172). If this is true, then the center of his philosophy is about recognizing the authority of the Other, and this is done by breaking the secret of Gyges, since it is Gyges' secret that allows us to be invisible to that authority. So it is that the Gyges question lies at the heart of Levinas's project. It becomes important in understanding Levinas, then, to understand how it was that he thought we might break Gyges' secret and become visible to the unique face of the Other.

Breaking the Secret by Opposing Gyges?

The first option for breaking the secret of Gyges might appear to be simply opposing Gyges or resisting his power in any way possible. When one unjustly becomes invisible to others and uses that invisibility to oppress others, opposing those invisible powers certainly seems desirable. As we saw in chapter 4, however, Levinas does not think that a mere reversal of Gyges is the solution to the totalizing gaze of Gyges.

We saw that the way to oppose the unseen seer is not to replace him with the Epicurean statue that is seen but unseeing. Opposing the totalizing of Gyges by opposing sight (conception, theorizing) altogether would be to become "statues looking at one another with empty eyes, idols which, contrary to Gyges, are exposed and do not see" (TI, 222). In chapter 4, we dismissed several interpretations of Levinas because they failed the Gyges test.[26] The goal of this chapter is to see if it is possible to find a type of wisdom that passes that test. That is, can we find a type of wisdom that breaks the pattern of Gyges (the unseen seer) without becoming its opposite (the unseeing seen). Toward the purpose of finding a type of wisdom that passes the Gyges test, it will help to first explore why Levinas did not prescribe flat opposition to Gyges as the secret to breaking Gyges' secret.

In trying to understand why the Gyges model is not best replaced with the blind statue model, we get an important clue by noting that Levinas refers to statues of *Epicurean* gods. By drawing upon the notion of Epicurean gods (TI, 222), we can see that Levinas views mere opposition to totality as isolation. If one is simply opposed to thematizing of all kinds, then ultimately one is left in the lonely condition of the Epicurean god who is entirely isolated from human interaction. The Epicureans believed gods existed, but not gods who interacted with or were concerned in any way with humans. Rather, the Epicurean "gods dwell in the *intermundia*, beautiful and happy and without thought of human affairs."[27] Their existence was entirely separate and unaffected by humans. Thus, to oppose totalizing by means of a mere reversal would be to isolate oneself such that communication and interaction are impossible. One can quickly see how isolation is not conducive to the ethical relation, since it precludes any relation whatsoever. Absolute otherness points to the uniqueness of the Other and the inability of the Other to be fully reduced to my categories of conception. But absolute otherness conceived of as a prohibition on speech and thought would make me absolutely separated from the other—an isolated Epicurean god. Absolute otherness cannot mean absolute separation because that would undermine the very ethical relation that recognizes the uniqueness of the other.

Another way to explain why Levinas does not prescribe a mere opposition to totalizing is to show the contradiction that such a position would make Levinas's entire project. To oppose totality on the basis of plurality is simply to support plurality on the foundation of plurality. Yet, he clearly wants to avoid this, as we see when he says that opposing totality for the sake of opposition would commit one to the error of having "a foundation of pluralism" (OB, 221). As we soon shall see, Levinas does not think that the foundation of pluralism should be pluralism itself. The foundation of pluralism is the ethical relation—being for the other. And this ethical relation must be more than simply resisting Gyges.

If one 'wages peace' by simply opposing violence, one has not tapped the root of the ethical relation. The opposition of violence is good, but opposition cannot be the foundation of opposition. Rather, being *for* the Other amounts to much more than simply being *against* the other's oppressor. Magda Trocmé gave testimony to this fact when she summed up her years of helping the Jews during the German occupation of France, saying simply that "*helping* Jews was more important than *resisting* Vichy and the Nazis."[28] More important than breaking Gyges directly is breaking his secret. So how is that done?

Breaking the Gyges Secret

Gyges' secret is broken by answering Gyges' question differently than Gyges answered it. In response to the question of whether it is better to suffer injustice or inflict it, Gyges answers that it is better to inflict injustice. Herodotus's Gyges[29] becomes invisible to the queen by raising the question of whether it is better to do injustice to the queen or suffer injustice himself. It is said that "Gyges, not being able to do otherwise, consented" to spy on the queen.[30] To say that he "was not able to do otherwise" says if he were to do otherwise, he would be suffering justice rather than inflicting it. Herodotus' Gyges[31] again becomes invisible—this time to the king—by raising the same question. This time it is in the form of asking, "Is it better to suffer unjust death or kill unjustly?" Herodotus writes that "he had no choice but to bring about his own death or the king's."

Plato's Gyges[32] is used in the context of asking whether it is better to suffer or inflict injustice. So what would be a sign that the secret had been broken? Would it be merely the absence of unjust violence? No. As we saw in the previous section, the wisdom of love seeks more than just opposing violence. We can tell that Gyges' secret has been broken when we see that someone chooses to suffer injustice instead of inflicting it. This is implicit throughout the corpus, and is at times stated explicitly. For example, Levinas addresses this directly in his important essay "Ethics as First Philosophy," saying that what is central to the ethical relation is "preferring to suffer than to commit injustice" and that recognizing this yields "suffering injustice rather than doing injustice" (85). So this question clearly plays a role in Levinas's work. Looking more closely, we may even discover that this question plays a *central* role. Levinas writes that "[t]he human is the return to the interiority of non-intentional consciousness, to bad conscience, to the possibility of its fearing injustice more than death, of preferring injustice suffered to injustice committed" (PT, 29). Choosing to suffer injustice over committing it is not just some supererogatory feat for some super saint. It is not just a mark of a highly ethical person. Levinas says preferring injustice suffered to injustice committed is what it means to be human.

Surely he is being hyperbolic, one might suggest. But what if we took this literally? How could one possibly answer the Gyges question in this way? The key to answering the question in favor of suffering, according to Levinas, is to remember the ethical relation that is part of my origin. That is, I must remember the fundamental fact that I am primordially responsible for the Other more than for myself. An immediate objection to this claim, however, is that there is no proof that this accurately describes my origin. I would agree that there is no absolute proof for this account of our origin, but there is, nonetheless, evidence that can be offered in favor of this account.[33] It could be argued that when self-deception is minimized, then the obvious fact of one's responsibility for the Other becomes undeniable. The testimony of the Chambonnais supports this view.

If one takes the view that we are each a collection of self-interests and that political gatherings only emerge out of a desire for self-preservation, it would be irrational for one to risk one's own life for the sake of protecting another. Thus, the Chambonnais were asked with incredulity why they acted in this strange way. The Chambonnais, however, did not see it as strange; they shrugged their shoulders, and asked, "where else could they go? I had to take them in." The fact that the Chambonnais saw their actions as perfectly ordinary provides evidence that it is in fact perfectly ordinary to be more for the Other than for oneself. They will "tell you that they are not morally better than anyone else." These humans believed and acted on the basic fact that life was precious, even though they could not prove this deductively. "For those who believe in the absolute preciousness of life there is no proof that the feelings and images and beliefs involved in such a belief are correct or even plausible. They can only *show* their beliefs." They showed this by refusing to "give up a life for any price—for their own comfort, for their own safety, for patriotism, or for legality."[34]

As these people explained later to Hallie, there are just some facts that are plain and without proof. One of these plain facts was that "it is better to help than to hurt." The Chambonnais did nothing to hide this fact from themselves, and acted in ways to help them remember the fact that it is better to help than to hurt. In contrast, the Nazi doctors used many layers of deception to hide this fact from themselves. The degree of self-deception at work in the individuals and groups played a significant role in whether one responded to the authority of the other. The beliefs that life is priceless and that it is better to help than to hurt "do their work in us: and when they fail, we know, when we do not manage to deceive ourselves, that they have failed to work in us."[35] These cases give evidence that this primordial responsibility is a true fact about us as humans.

But of course, it can be objected that if this infinite responsibility for the Other occurs only when there are just two, and there is always a third, then I never find myself in this primordial situation where there is just the Other and myself. If I never find myself in this primordial situation, then why does such an account of my origin make any difference? How is this different from a Hobbesian wisdom built on the presupposition that, primordially, we are basically and properly autonomous and self-interested? If a democratic state can be properly based on either account of human origin, then what practical difference does it make, and how is the Levinasian account providing anything new, let alone radical?

Perhaps anticipating such objections, Levinas wrote, "it is then not without importance to know if the egalitarian and just State in which man is fulfilled . . . proceeds from a war of all against all, or from the irreducible responsibility of the one for all, and if it can do without friendship and faces" (OB, 159–60). So Levinas shows that he thinks it is important to know the origin of wisdom and politics, but why is it important?

§7 Forms of Speaking with Wisdom of Love

Although Levinas addresses it with understatement, the answer is that know-ing the origin of wisdom is important because it affects the way we speak—it affects the way we treat our neighbor. Although a wisdom of love and a love of wisdom may in many respects look alike in day-to-day democracy, these two types of speaking are in fact worlds apart. There may be few dis-tinguishable differences when observing how each type of politics votes on building a new sewage treatment plant. But the differences are most clearly revealed in situations of crisis—situations when one is faced with choosing between two or more injustices. What, then, are the ways of speaking that are compatible with a wisdom of love? Again, Levinas does not present these ways in a clear or systematic way, but reading across his corpus, we can iden-tify three primary modes of speaking in wisdom of love. These include prophecy, teaching, and testimony. But these forms of speech have a special-ized meaning for Levinas.

Prophecy

Looking first at prophecy, it might come as no surprise to say that Levinas encourages prophecy as a form of speech that is compatible with wisdom of love. Westphal underscores this point by summarizing that "Levinas places his philosophy in the prophetic tradition."[36] Derrida also draws attention to this prophetic quality of Levinas's speech. Derrida describes Levinas's philos-ophy as moving "toward a prophetic speech." Derrida contrasts Levinas's prophetic speech with prophecy that comes from a Greek source, saying that Levinas's prophecy draws from "a more ancient volcano."[37] And in fact, I would argue that Derrida is partly right. Derrida is right, in my view, to say that Levinas is suggesting a prophetic speech, and that it draws from a more ancient (that is, Jewish) source. This is supported when Levinas asks the question, "What difference is there between institutions arising from a lim-itation of violence and those arising from a limitation of responsibility?" He answers that by saying, "There is, at least, this one: in the second case, one can revolt against institutions in the very name of that which gave birth to them" (GDT, 183). So Derrida is right that Levinas encourages prophetic speech, but it is a different sort of prophecy than what Derrida has in mind. It is not so much prophetic speech that revolts by scorching the earth and all its institutions. Rather, it is a prophetic speech that speaks most clearly by throwing itself into the volcano.

What I mean is this: Levinas, unlike Derrida, does not say that all speech is violence and that the best we can hope for is the violence of prophecy used against the greater violence of totality. The wisdom and politics and speech that are made necessary by the entry of the third are not just of a different degree than what they displace. Rather, Levinas holds that this prophetic speech is qualitatively different from the violence it challenges. There are two types of revolt—one may revolt against injustice in the name of my self-interest, but one may also revolt against injustice in the name of responsibility for the other. As the above quote suggests, the difference between these two types of revolt is seen most clearly in moments of crisis—and especially when the crisis is a dilemma of the Gyges sort, where it is a raw choice between an injustice against your self-interest or an injustice against mine. If the origin of justice is self-interest, then one may answer Gyges' question in a way that justifies injustice to the other. However, if one appeals to a different origin—one of responsibility for the other—then Gyges' question is answered quite differently. With the appeal to original responsibility, I will answer that it is better for me to suffer than to inflict injustice.

We see a little more clearly how Levinas envisions this prophetic speech in his essay "Uniqueness." He says that even though politics, wisdom, and the judgments of justice may be necessary once there is a third, these systems of thought "cannot make us forget the origin of the right or the uniqueness of the other" (UN, 196). Prophetic voices are those that bring this to the attention of those in these institutions. Politics and wisdom of institutions "cannot abandon that uniqueness to political history, which is engaged in the determinism of powers, reasons of state, totalitarian temptations and complacencies. It awaits the voices that will recall, to the judgments of the judges and statesmen, the human face dissimulated beneath the identities of citizens." He identifies this speech as prophetic, saying, "Perhaps these are the 'prophetic voices'" (UN, 196).

But as we have already seen,[38] Levinas is not advocating mere resistance, as is the form that much prophecy takes. So how does one actually speak prophetically against an institution without resorting to merely scorching it with prophetic speech? An example of prophetic speech by the Chambonnais would be the way in which they helped the Jews without directly opposing the Nazis. They felt no loyalty to government, but still thought it important to respect government authorities in areas that did not contradict the command to love their neighbor. Therefore, they did not directly oppose or resist. In fact when government officials visited Le Chambon, the Chambonnais gave them the minimally due respect but went no further than that. They did not throw grenades or even tomatoes, but neither did they hang flags or provide lavish food. "If they had tried to confront their opponents publicly, there would have been no contest, only immediate and total defeat." Even while giving the officials their due respect, the Chambonnais handed the officer a letter, which in part read: "We feel obliged to tell you that there are among us a certain number of Jews. But, we make no distinction between Jews and non-Jews. It is contrary to the Gospel teaching." The letter was respectful, but stated clearly, "If our comrades . . . received the order to let themselves be deported . . . we would try to hide them as best we could."[39]

Two weeks later, the police came to round up the Jews he knew were being hidden there. The Chambonnais refused to turn them over, but they continued to show the minimal courtesy duty required. The police brought gray buses to haul away the Jews, but found only one. So while the search continued, this one young half-Jew sat alone in one of the buses, and then the townspeople started bringing him generous portions of their rationed food and passing it through the window to him. They did not start a riot or attack the police. Their actions of giving food to that one prisoner were prophecy of the sort I am speaking about in this section. Amazingly, the officer released the prisoner on a technicality[40] before driving away with empty buses. This is the prophetic speech that belongs to the wisdom of love—it is prophecy without resistance. It is qualitatively different.

Teaching

Another sort of speaking that belongs to the wisdom of love is teaching. But here again, we must look at the exact use of this term as it applies here. This is a term Levinas uses frequently in *Totality and Infinity*, but infrequently elsewhere in his corpus. It is nonetheless instructive in revealing the type of speech Levinas thought was possible.[41]

We see that teaching is a type of language—even a type of thematizing, when Levinas writes that "[t]eaching . . . is a thematization" (TI, 99). Here again, we see that wisdom of love is not mere silence. Even though it opposes certain types of totalizing speech, wisdom of love is "in contrast with the silent world, ambiguity infinitely magnified, stagnant water, water stilled with mystification that passes for mystery." Instead, the "proposition relates the phenomenon to the existent, to exteriority, to the Infinity of the Other

uncontained by my thought" (TI, 99). We see in this description a hint as
to why the silence of mere opposition is undesirable. If I were to do nothing
but oppose thematizing, my only logical position would be one of silence,
and that would be a position that was unrelated to the Other. But teaching
allows for speech with the Other without 'containing' the Other in my conceptual reductions of him.

But what can we say more specifically about teaching as a positive form
of speech? There are three things I want to point out about teaching: first,
teaching is not violent. Second, teaching does not come from within me as
in the Platonic model of recollection. Third, teaching is what I receive from
the Other as a gift. I receive from the Other something entirely new. I will
say more about each of these three points.

The first and most obvious observation to make about teaching echoes
what has been said of prophecy—namely, this form of speech is not violent.
It is "fundamentally pacific" and it is a "mastery that does not conquer, but
teaches" (TI, 71). It is not that teaching is the least violent of all types of
speech, which is necessarily violent. Rather, teaching is qualitatively different from violent types of speech. "Teaching is not a species of a genus called
domination, a hegemony at work within a totality, but is the presence of
infinity breaking the closed circle of totality" (TI, 171).

Second, learning is not something that arises from within me or my
memory. Socrates made an advance by envisioning teaching as midwifery, as
opposed to the seductive and violent forms of speech practiced by the
sophists. Levinas even says that "[t]his whole work [i.e., TI]" seeks to present
the ethical as prior to the Socratic dialogue since it presupposes that the interlocutors have accepted the rules of dialogue. Teaching, as Levinas describes it,
comes before that assent—before I can give my cooperation, and thus "teaching leads to the logical discourse without rhetoric, without flattery or seduc-
tion and hence without violence" (TI, 180). Levinas argued that teaching is
more than a Socratic maieutic. Teaching "does not merely assume an after all
subsidiary function of being midwife to a mind already pregnant with its
fruit" (TI, 98). The reason for this is that a merely maieutic model of teaching allows for learning to be derived from that which is within me already.
But in contrast to this, the Other is able to provide me with something that
was not already in me. "Teaching is a way for truth to be produced such that
it is *not my work*, such that I could not derive it from my own interiority" (TI,
295; my emphasis). So teaching is not fundamentally from me.

The third point is that teaching comes from the Other. Levinas is using
a technical sense of the word teaching, because when he uses the term, his
emphasis is on the way in which I am taught, rather than on how I teach.

Welcoming the Other is "to *receive* from the Other beyond the capacity of the I, which means exactly: to have the idea of infinity. But this also means: to be taught" (TI, 51; emphasis in original). The Other can call me into question, and this can seem hostile, but "inasmuch as it is welcomed this conversation is a teaching [*enseignement*]" (TI, 51). Since I am welcoming it, this speech is a "nonviolent transitivity" and this teaching is neither the coercive persuasion of the sophists, nor the recollecting maieutics of Socrates, but it is a nonviolent receiving of something new—something not anticipated or already possessed by the student. "Teaching is a discourse in which the master can bring to the student what the student does not yet know" (TI, 180). And of course, the Other is not preparing a lecture and then giving it to me. But that which is taught comes from the Other herself. The "whole infinity of exteriority is not first produced, to then teach: teaching is its very production. The first teaching teaches this very height, tantamount to its exteriority, the ethical" (TI, 171).

That teaching is appropriate to the wisdom of love as described from the perspective of the student shows that this wisdom is not the sort of wisdom whose defining mark is the possessing of wisdom that can be dispensed. Rather, this view of wisdom is not unlike the biblical person of wisdom who has an unexpected relationship to rebuke. "[T]he wise, when rebuked, will love you."[42] The mark of wisdom is not the ability to give rebuke but the ability to receive it. Rebuke is an appropriate term for what Levinas is describing here since the Other calls me into question. It is the Other who is my teacher in the sense of being my master who has authority that comes from a 'height' and this "voice coming from another shore teaches transcendence itself" (TI, 171). And even though this may again seem violent and in violation of my freedom, it is nonetheless capable of being ignored or disobeyed. The Other teaches the wise, and that wisdom comes not from within the wise but from the Other and this teaching "continues the placing in me of the idea of infinity" (TI, 180).

Testimony

Most revealing of all the forms of speech is testimony, and like prophecy and teaching, testimony is not used in an entirely ordinary way. Testimony is bearing witness to the infinity of the Other. The infinite responsibility that this entails could be denied or ignored, but I testify to that infinity by saying simply, "here I am!" (me voici). In so doing I am acknowledging that this infinity exists in the Other.

I began this section[43] by asking how it is that one can answer Gyges'
question in favor of suffering rather than in favor of inflicting injustice. If I
must speak, how can I speak without answering that I will inflict rather than
suffer injustice? It is in this testimony that we speak in favor of the Other.
"When in the presence of the Other, I say 'Here I am!', this 'Here I am!' is
the place through which the infinite enters into language" (GT, 106). To say
'Here I am!' is to echo many of the biblical prophets and those called by
God.[44] It is to admit exposure, and to come out of hiding.

This bearing witness which says 'Here I am' breaks Gyges' secret which
itself is the veil of invisibility. It refuses to hide behind the deception that I
am designed as one who is basically self-interested. Rather, it comes out of
hiding. I can hide behind self-preservation and pretend that I am not originally responsible for the Other, but that does not change the fact that I am
in fact responsible for the Other. By testifying my presence before the Other,
the secret of Gyges is broken, and "[c]ontrary to Gyges, who sees without
being seen, here I am seen without seeing" (GDT, 196). Here is the only
place Levinas endorses a mere reversal of Gyges—that is, "being seen without seeing." But if there is always a third, then when can I ever say "Here I
am!"? He still acknowledges that this only occurs in the original relation
(when there are only two) saying that testimony "is not thematized, in any
case originally" (GT, 106). But as we have seen, there is, in fact, always a
third; so how can I give testimony in this sense? Without denying that there
is always a third, we can nonetheless find times when it is as if there are only
two. When the first German Jew came to Magda Trocmé's door, "ethics
became incarnate" and "[o]nly then were *two* individual human beings
involved: one in danger, and one being asked to help."[45] Despite the fact,
therefore, that there is always a third, there are nonetheless existential situations which closely approximate that primordial situation of the original ethical relation.

And I can find myself in this primordial situation by conceptual con-
struction. The Gyges question is usually framed in terms of just two. Even
though there are others capable of being placed into the equation, the Gyges
question is posed in terms of "it's me or you." So the possibility of 'just two'
still occurs within one's concepts that are raised precisely to provide me cover
from the Other. "One would prefer . . . to take refuge in one's concept in
which the limits of obligation are found" (GDT, 196). And it is precisely in
this situation where testimony breaks Gyges' secret and removes that veil
which I use to hide myself from responsibility.

It is in these existential or conceptual encounters of just one Other that
Gyges' question potentially has the greatest effect. Yet, it is precisely in these

encounters where testimony speaks only of my vulnerable exposure before the face of the Other. In bearing witness, "there is no refuge for this subject in the secrecy that would protect him from [responsibility for] the neighbor" (GDT, 195). In this "bearing witness, there is not recovery of self by self; there is neither shelter nor screen" (GDT, 196). Gyges' question is like the "thickets of Paradise where Adam hid upon hearing the voice of the Eternal" but just as for Adam, hiding does not remove one's responsibility. Bearing witness simply acknowledges that responsibility by removing the deceptive hiding. It "is a question of an exposure without shelter, as under a leaden sun without protective shade" where escape becomes impossible—it is an "exposure without reserve" (GDT, 196).

It seems clear then that testimony "brings me out of invisibility" (OB, 150). And what are the words of the testimony? "It is the 'here I am'" that helps break "the bad silence that shelters the secret of Gyges" (GCM, 75). But what can be said more specifically about this testimony? It is not ordinary testimony. This bearing witness is not a mere pointing to some other experience, but the very act of saying "here I am!" is both testimony and that about which is being testified. This "witness is not reducible to the relationship that leads from an index to the indicated" (OB, 151). The Infinite, according to Levinas, does not show itself in a theme, but in "the one who bears witness to it; it is the witnessing that belongs to the glory of the Infinite" and it "is by the voice of the witness that the glory of the Infinite is witnessed" (GDT, 197). One interviewer of Levinas responded with surprise, "but wait: who testifies to what and to whom in testimony?" And Levinas responded to this question saying, "you continue here to think of testimony as based on knowledge and thematization. The concept of testimony I am trying to describe surely implies a mode of revelation" (GT, 107). What, then, does this testimony reveal? It reveals another secret—the very secret that breaks Gyges' secret. "The 'Here I am' . . . is the secret of sociality" which is "the 'love of my neighbor'" (NC, 131).[46] In other words, the testimony, which is a vulnerable response to the Other by the ego, is itself a testimony to the secret of sociality, which is the fact that the ego is vulnerable to and responsible to the Other.

This treatment of testimony has been executed with the purpose of showing that nonviolent speech is possible, and it seems clear enough that testimony so described does, in fact, refrain from violence to the Other. What is not immediately evident, however, is how this testimony avoids making the one who testifies a victim of violence himself. If it is a mere reversal of violence, then the violent word still has the last word. A hint of an answer is given on the final page of *Otherwise than Being*, in which

Levinas writes that each individual "is called to leave in his turn . . . the concept of the ego . . . to respond with responsibility . . . and say *here I am for the others,* to lose his place . . . or his shelter" (OB, 185; emphasis in original). On one hand the "here I am for the others" which causes one to lose his place and shelter seems utterly hostile to that individual, but when we understand that it is a 'call' that one can ignore, then we can see how it is not entirely involuntary. It may be initially involuntary in that the call is made without our consent, and I cannot alter the fact that I am so called. But volition has its place in that I have the power to either ignore or respond to that call. The "here I am" is one response to that call, but another response to that call could be to simply remain hidden. If Levinas held that the responsibility for the Other was an entirely involuntary obligation, then the following statement of Levinas's would be in contradiction to that. He says that "my passivity breaks out in saying: 'Here I am!' The exteriority of the Infinite somehow becomes 'interiority' in the sincerity of the testimony" (GT, 109). That the exteriority could become interiority does not make sense if exteriority is absolutely contrary to interiority.

Why then is it coherent to say that exteriority of the infinite becomes interiority in testimony? It is coherent because testimony involves the freedom of the ego, which chooses to present itself nonsurreptitiously to the Other. One either chooses to be a slave to the pursuit of hiding from the Other, or one chooses to stop hiding from the Other and be responsible for the Other. If I choose to be responsible for the Other, then how is this at all different from the social contract anthropology Levinas opposes? I cannot choose to be responsible for the Other, such that my responsibility can be traced ultimately to *my* choice—an implicit or explicit contract that I made. Rather, the idea here is more complex. The freedom involved is a choice to stop hiding from a responsibility that called me and claimed me before I even had the opportunity to choose. My *responsibility* for the Other is not traced to my choice, but the *hiding* is indeed traced to my choice. Thus, exteriority can become interiority when I choose to cease my free pursuit of evasion and invisibility.

This helps us understand why testimony is not my saying, "Hey, let me tell you about this Other." If that were the case, then I would be eliminating the exteriority of the Other by representing him to you as a concept. Rather, I am testifying to testifying. "The witness testifies to what was said by himself. For he has said 'Here I am!' before the Other; and from the fact that before the Other he recognizes the responsibility which is incumbent on himself, he has manifested what the face of the Other signified for him" (GT, 109). To do the former is say that I know what the Other is, and to reduce the Other to a derivation of my conception. To do the latter is simply to say that the Other is beyond my conception; the response to the Other as such is simply to say, "Here I am." In the latter case, I do not annihilate my interiority because of my testimony, but neither do I deny the exteriority of the Other, because I am merely presenting myself to him. In this sense, the witness who so testifies becomes a revelation[47] of the Other because the "glory of the Infinite reveals itself through what it is capable of doing in the witness" (GT, 109).

Of course, "Here am I!" is merely one possible locution for this testimony. Levinas offers another example, saying that testimony may be "as simple as 'hello'" (TDT, 103). No doubt, and without proof, another example of testimony was the simple phrase, "Naturally, come in, and come in."[48]

Chapter 6

The Scales of Wisdom

Having examined the way in which Gyges' secret can be broken, there remains one last question to address which bears significantly on our topic of the wisdom of love. If wisdom and politics are necessary, as I have argued, then is there anything that can be said about the external conditions of our political and societal gatherings as they relate to the possibility of keeping or breaking Gyges' secret? Are there conditions conducive to keeping Gyges' secret and are there conditions conducive to breaking that secret? I will argue that the scale of our gatherings affects the type of wisdom that is practiced. I will suggest that the smaller-sized gatherings are conducive to the wisdom of love, whereas larger-sized collectives are more conducive to a politics of invisibility.

§1 Large-scale Wisdom

Although Levinas does not address the issue of the scale of political gathering and its effect on visibility or invisibility to the Other, he does suggest that necessary wisdom is not a wisdom of love when it becomes a politics administered anonymously or when the political society becomes an end unto itself. I will look briefly at these features as Levinas treats them before suggesting that politics on larger scales are more conducive to these anonymous, self-serving states which help to sustain Gyges' secret rather than break it.

As early as *Totality and Infinity*, Levinas identified anonymity as a mark of a politics that is inhuman. The mark of the tyrannous state is that instead

123

of endorsing a truth, "which should reconcile persons," it "exists anonymously" (46). This tyranny, which exists as a "faceless generous mother" is "neutralizing" and "remains obedient to the anonymous" (45–46). Though the term 'anonymity' appears early in the corpus, Levinas continues to speak of the tyranny of the anonymous wisdom in *Otherwise than Being*, and in essays and interviews in his later works.[1]

After admitting that the third party calls for the necessity of politics, society, and philosophy as wisdom of love, he is quick to add the qualification that the "justice, society and truth itself which they require, must not be taken for an anonymous law of the 'human forces' governing an impersonal totality" (OB, 161). He continues making this important qualification when he admits the necessity of politics. In "Peace and Proximity," for example, Levinas explains how being-for-the-Other leads to the necessity of 'political laws' after the 'third party' is introduced. But again, he immediately qualifies this by adding that the set of political laws should not be seen as a "natural and anonymous legality regulating human masses" (143). The reason for this is that an anonymous legality defaces the human. To depersonalize politics is to dehumanize the state. If we must judge, we must judge, but this necessity need not cause us to replace judges with abstract rules that do not see the unique face of the Other. "What is inhuman is to be judged without anyone who judges" (IT, 31). The necessity of judging does not justify going beyond what is necessary. "When more than two come together and the 'being-together' of humans is organized out of necessity, one can tell that the administration of this organizing has gone "beyond these necessities" when they appeal to "abstract rules . . . in the name of anonymous powers" (US, 114).

The consequence of such anonymous domination is that the "communitarian ends of the group are forgotten" (US, 114). This comment helps lead us to the indicator of a political wisdom that has crossed the line of necessary organization to dominating rule. When a political state begins to see itself as its own end, the necessary state has forgotten its purpose for coming into existence, which is to make judgments about how to divide our responsibility between the Other and the third. If a State becomes "abandoned to its own necessity" (PP, 144), then anything is justified for the sake of the State, and this can be used to help keep Gyges' secret, thereby unnecessarily limiting my responsibility for the Other. To the contrary, the "responsibility of 'one for the Other'" is what "delimits the State and ceaselessly calls for the watchfulness of persons, who cannot content themselves with the simple subsuming of cases beneath the general rule, as the computer is capable of doing" (PP, 144). When the State forgets that it was formed out of the need to serve the unique

Other, the "State structures [set] themselves up as ends in themselves" and in so doing contribute to the "deterioration of social relations" (US, 116).

I here want to suggest that there is one condition which has not been emphasized by Levinas, but which plays a significant role in the degree to which an organization or societal gathering either moves toward anonymous regulation or toward the recognition of the unique human face. That variable is the condition of scale, and the question I wish to raise is how the size of the group affects the wisdom that is at work in the judgments made by those in the group. Are large political groupings more conducive to this anonymous sort of governing, which in turn sustains the secret of Gyges? And is the corollary of this true as well? Are small political groupings more conducive to governing which recognizes the unique face of the Other and thereby helps break the secret of Gyges? It is unlikely that we could claim a necessary causal relationship, since the counterexamples of small faceless groups and large non-anonymous groups could easily disprove such a causal link. However, it could also be true that the multiplicity of causes in our lived experience is such that there are other factors that cause the exceptions. It is conceivable that all other factors being equal, the smaller society will always be more humane than the larger. I am not prepared to defend such a claim of necessary causation, but neither am I prepared to ignore the possibility of a positive correlation, since it is potentially one of the factors over which we have the greatest ability to contribute directly to the breaking or keeping of Gyges' secret.

What reason might there be for thinking that there is a positive correlation between the size of the group and the tendency of that group to embrace an anonymous legality? One reason is the simple empirical fact that relates to our field of vision. The closer a person's face is to my view, the more space that person's face occupies in my field of vision. For example, in order to have a thousand faces in my view at once, each face would, at the most, occupy 1/1000 or one tenth of one percent of my field of vision. If I am looking at the face of just one other person, then that face could occupy almost one hundred percent of my visual field. Another reason is seen when we expand Levinas's analysis of the Other and the third to a fourth, fifth, or sixth person. We have seen what a difference the addition of the Third makes in my need to make comparisons and judgments in order to divide my responsibilities between these two Others. But with each addition of a unique Other, my sense of responsibility becomes less immediate, and more reliant on my theoretical reasoning.

I know a person who hails from rural Arkansas and is as attendant to the needs of the Other as almost anyone I have met. I took him to see New York

City for the first time and he was extremely anxious the entire time we were in the city. I assured him we were quite safe from harm, but he assured me that was not his worry. He was not afraid that something would happen to him—he was simply overwhelmed with the mass of faces. It is possible that he is so attentive to the needs of individual Others, that upon seeing this mass of faces, he became overwhelmed by the implications this had on his sense of responsibility to these people. Most experienced urbanites had already learned what he had not—they had learned to ignore the faces of the masses. They had learned not to look people in the eye—not to say hello. They had learned to develop a certain invisibility to the masses. If I walk down the streets of a small town of 500, it is rare to pass someone on the sidewalk without being greeted personally along with a look in the eye. Is it that those in large cities are just less friendly to passersby? Or is it that the large number of people with whom they are in association compels them to put up these protective defenses? Does the large size push us toward an anonymous interaction with the Other? Zygmunt Bauman seems to think so, suggesting that rather than deny our neighbor, we hide ourselves from him, which is easier to do in a large city. "Keeping the neighbours at arm's length prevents us from having to make the choice."[2]

Testing this correlation on the Holocaust supports the idea that the size of the group directly affects our ability to become invisible to our neighbor. An early stage in the process was forcing the Jews to leave their normal domiciles where they were literally the neighbor next door. They were forced to live in Jewish ghettos where those looking at them could much more easily hide from the individuality of the Other because they were easy to dehumanize in a mass. And of course, they were then 'concentrated' even further, which further facilitated the task of hiding. It is easier to keep on a mask when the victim is gathered en masse. It is easier to disappear from a mass million than it is to disappear from one or two faces.[3]

§2 Small-scale Wisdom

Levinas did not speak very often on this topic, and when he did, he did not speak long, but at least we can see that he hinted in the direction of the smallness of wisdom of love. On multiple occasions he refers to Vassily Grossman, who "thinks that the 'small goodness' from one person to his fellowman is lost and deformed as soon as it seeks organization and universality and system." Unbeaten, this 'small goodness' "undergoes the violence of evil, which, as small goodness, it can neither vanquish nor drive out. A little kindness going only from man to man" (OUJ, 230). Levinas goes on further about Grossman saying that this small goodness or 'little kindness' is described as "beautiful and powerless, like the dew" (PO, 109). Examples of this little kindness included "the kindness of a soldier who holds his canteen out to a wounded enemy. The kindness of youth taking pity on old age, the kindness of a peasant who hides an old Jew in his barn."[4]

One may object to this sort of conclusion about the smallness of goodness—the scale of wisdom of love at the service of love. If we say that wisdom carried out in small-scale settings is more conducive to neighbor-love than wisdom carried out in large-scale settings, one might fear, as Davenport voices, the "privatization of agape." He criticizes Levinas for emphasizing the particular Other so much that he is "insufficiently attentive to the fact that in some cases we can also love others as our neighbors without directly encountering them in the flesh, or face-to-face, as Levinas puts it."[5] This is a healthy fear since Levinas might be interpreted as attending to the local neighbor while ignoring the global neighbor. We can, however, hear the Other,[6] which allows for the possibility of being called into question by someone with whom I am not face-to-face. Furthermore, the allowance of politics and justice makes possible many types of political solutions to the suffering of others, and does not preclude institutions that are designed to serve others. But despite these caveats, Levinas's emphasis still remains focused on the particular Other. Perhaps Levinas is right in holding that it is more important to love particular humans than humanity in general. Levinas would disagree with Nietzsche, who thought that "higher than love of the neighbor is love of the farthest."[7] It is precisely this love for the farthest—for the universal everyone—that can undermine our love for the neighbor. Perhaps a way to respond to the call of the farthest is to go be physically near to them.[8]

This variable of scale leads us back to the examples of the people who lived in the small village of Le Chambon at the time of the war. The village was small enough that they all knew each other, and the entire village (led by the example of Andre Trocmé) was convinced of their need to help those who came to them seeking refuge. I have already spoken of their example, so need not say much more, except that their scale of encountering the Jews was in sharp contrast to the scale on which the Nazis encountered them. The Chambonnais hid these refugees in the houses that lay at the edges of the town near forests, and when Nazis would come seeking to capture the refugees, the Chambonnais would send them into the forest. They were dispersed throughout the village and would be dispersed even further when police came searching for them. The Nazis were doing just the opposite. While the Chambonnais were scattering refugees, the Nazis were *concentrating* them. Thus the Chambonnais saw the Jews in small numbers and the Nazis saw them gathered in masses. It could be argued that the deconcentration of the refugees had an effect even on the Nazis whose job it was to find these refugees. On one occasion, a gendarme thought he had stumbled across a Jew and told him to run away quickly because more police were coming.[9] I wonder what that gendarme might have done if he had encountered the same person as just one more face in the midst of hundreds of captives in a concentration camp? To what degree was this gendarme's impulse to help the Jew escape a result of his finding him alone—one on one? Was it easier to save him since it was just the two of them there?

The account given by the Chambonnais certainly suggests that the smallness of number impacted their choices. When the first German Jew first came to Magda Trocmé's door, "ethics became incarnate" and "[o]nly then were two individual human beings involved: one in danger, and one being asked to help." There were no statues erected, and this place is not visited the way the battlefields are visited. "[F]rom the point of view of historians, something small had happened here." But that is precisely my point—on the historical scale of numbers and significance of world events, this was in fact small. But it might be that this was one of the greatest events in France during that time, and that it was possible precisely because its scale was so statistically small. The people in this town quickly became united in their commitment to risk their lives by hiding the refugees, and this congealing took place both in the church and around kitchen tables. Hallie called it a "kitchen struggle."[10] If any monuments are erected, they should be erected on a kitchen table.

Chalmers, the Quaker, played a key role in helping give confidence to these people's conviction. Perhaps Chalmers was drawing upon his knowledge of the Quaker experience with the underground railroad during the U.S. Civil War (which involved an informal collection of families who harbored runaway slaves on their route to freedom in the North). It is often said of the Quakers that they have had "a vital social impact far in excess of their numbers."[11] Perhaps, however, their great influence was not *in spite* of their small numbers, but partly *because* of those numbers.

Lifton also gives examples of those within Germany who actively undermined the Nazi project. Although the majority of churches allied themselves to the National Socialist regime, the smaller body who called themselves the "Confessional Church" worked effectively to stall, in the early years of the regime, the movement to systematically and medically kill the mentally ill. Lifton concluded that "this Nazi attempt at medical mystification of killing was given the lie . . . by a few church leaders, who gave voice to the grief and rage of victimized families with ethical passions stemming from their own religious traditions."[12] This was not a large opposition force, but a few leaders and a few churches responding to the plight of a few victims.[13]

It is not uncommon upon arriving at a meeting for prayer that only draws together a handful of participants, to hear someone say, "For where two or three are gathered in my name, I am there among them."[14] When this is cited in such a context, the implication usually is that where there are *at least* two or three who come together, God is present there. But that is not how it reads. It reads, simply, "For where two or three are gathered in my name, I am there among them." Perhaps this is further testimony to the importance of small-scale gatherings.

Philosopher and novelist Wendell Berry writes in his novel *Jayber Crow* about a small town, Port William, in which the barber, Jayber Crow, comes to see that the town helps constitute who he is as a self—as a moral self. In considering the consequences of the war that the country was entering, he reflected on the difference between the nation and the own small town to whom he was responsible. "No more can I think of Port William and the United States in the same thought," Jayber pondered. "A nation is an idea, and Port William is not. Maybe there is no live connection between a little place and a big idea. I think there is not." And then reflecting further on the scale of neighbor-love, he continues, "Did I think that the great organizations of the world could love their enemies? I did not. I didn't think great organizations could love anything."[15] This is not to say that organizations cannot do good, but he was not part of any large organization in the way that he was a part of his small community of Port William.

Perhaps it is in these smallest of gatherings—around kitchen tables, when someone comes to your door, and the like, when one is most fully exposed to the infinite. We are told that God hates unjust scales, and the scales are most literally scales used to measure, but in what way might it be possible that large scales are less just than small scales? And finally, if measuring is made necessary by the entrance of the third, I simply wonder in what ways a small scale may be better equipped to measure the infinite than the massive scale, at least in part because the small scale cannot pretend that it has in measuring a drop of water captured the sea.

Conclusion

Since Levinas advocates testimony as one type of speech consistent with the wisdom of love, I will testify[1] that in researching and writing this book, I have learned a secret—Gyges' secret. I have learned the importance of Gyges' question—how I have used it and how I might be tempted to use it—to clear my conscience. Levinas has taught me another secret, though. He has shown me the importance of breaking this secret, and the importance of becoming visible to others.

I once avoided the opportunity to choose a child to tutor because tutoring one child, after all, seemed a waste of time when that meant there would be thousands others I could not help. Besides, I was in graduate school, and it would be more important for me to stay cloistered, preparing myself to succeed in great acts of moral heroism. I have learned by reading the testimonial actions of Andre Trocmé that the way to prepare for grand acts of moral heroism includes practicing small acts of concern for my particular neighbor, and I have learned from reading Levinas that this is not the same as practicing random acts of kindness.

More concretely, I have learned from my neighbors that the Other chooses me, and that this is not random. Consider the following: school is out for the day, and Sam and DayDay[2]—two fatherless boys who live within sight—show up on my doorstep and ring my doorbell. I am studying. They ring again—longer this time. I suspect they will ask me, like always, "Whatcha doing, Corey? Can we do it too?" I have been chosen. I have been

131

called. And I become more human—less enslaved to my own autonomy—by walking down the stairs, opening the door, and saying, "here I am." This is very small, yet it is an opportunity to encounter the infinite.

I hope that if I am presented with a severe form of Gyges' question that I will respond as Magda Trocmé and say, "come in, come in." I hope that I will be willing to suffer injustice rather than inflict it. But I will be called in smaller ways many times before then, if then. In any case, this is my hope: I hope I will testify with a wisdom of love in the service of love.

Notes

Introduction

1   All texts by Levinas will be cited with abbreviations. See the list of abbreviations on page xi and following.

Chapter 1

1   This title is given by some since he is considered to be the founder of objective history. This is, of course, disputed, and he is even called the "father of lies" by some since it is not widely agreed that his histories were factual.

2   Herodotus, *Here Are Set Forth the Histories of Herodotus of Halicarnassus; That Men's Actions May Not in Time Be Forgotten nor Things Great and Wonderful, Accomplished Whether by Greeks or Barbarians, Go without Report, nor, Especially, the Cause of the Wars between One and the Other,* ed. Harry Graham Carter (New York: Heritage Press, 1959).

3   See Alain Finkielkraut, *The Wisdom of Love,* vol. 20, *Texts and Contexts* (Lincoln: University of Nebraska Press, 1997). See also Roger Burggraeve, *The Wisdom of Love in the Service of Love: Emmanuel Levinas on Justice, Peace, and Human Rights,* trans. Jeffrey Bloechl (Milwaukee: Marquette University Press, 2002). Burggraeve's book was not available when I was first reviewing the literature and writing the first draft of my manuscript. I only discovered his work after completing my own, and while I was pleased to find this fine piece of scholarship arguing for the possibility of Levinasian politics that is not fundamentally violent, I found that there were some significant points of disagreement, some of which I will identify here.

4   Finkielkraut, *Wisdom of Love*, 90–91.
5   Burggraeve, *Wisdom of Love in the Service of Love*, 140.
6   Finkielkraut, *Wisdom of Love*.
7   Burggraeve, *Wisdom of Love in the Service of Love*, 143.
8   In this book, I draw from texts from across the breadth of the Levinas corpus with the exception of the Jewish works. I originally did this because I think the interpretation I offer can be made without them, and I sought a primarily philosophical audience. But I find these works to be rich and valuable, and were I to now include them, it would only strengthen my argument.
9   Tamra Wright, *The Paradox of Morality* (New York: Routledge, 1988), 168–70.
10   Perhaps this deserves further treatment at some time in the future, but such a project exceeds the scope of this current book.

Chapter 2

1   Colin Davis, *Levinas: An Introduction* (Notre Dame, Ind.: University of Notre Dame Press, 1996), 5, 70.
2   Davis, *Levinas*, 37–38.
3   Robert Gibbs, "Review of *Ethics, Exegesis, and Philosophy: Interpretation after Levinas* by Richard Cohen," *Notre Dame Philosophical Reviews* (2002).
4   Perhaps his method of writing is not dissimilar to that of Flannery O'Connor as self-described when she wrote to a playwright friend, Maryat Lee, in a 1959 letter that the "thing to do is write something with a delayed reaction like those capsules that take an hour to melt in the stomach. In this way, it could be performed on Monday and not make them vomit until Wednesday, by which time they would not be sure who was to blame. This is the principle I operate under and I find it works very well." Flannery O'Connor and Sally Fitzgerald, *The Habit of Being: Letters* (New York: Vintage Books, 1980), 349.
5   Davis, *Levinas*, 71.
6   Jacques Derrida, "Violence and Metaphysics: An Essay on the Thought of Emmanuel Levinas," in *Writing and Difference,* ed. Alan Bass (Chicago: University of Chicago Press, 1978), 312.
7   Richard J. Bernstein, *The New Constellation: The Ethical-Political Horizons of Modernity/Postmodernity*, 1st ed. (Cambridge, Mass.: MIT Press, 1992), 71.
8   Simon Critchley and Robert Bernasconi, *The Cambridge Companion to Levinas* (Cambridge: Cambridge University Press, 2002), 6.
9   Davis, *Levinas*, 57.
10   "La philosophie: sagesse de l'amour au service de l'amour" (AE, 207).
11   Levinas is not systematic in his writing style, so he does not always offer clear definitions for terms, but where possible, I will try to provide statements that, if not completely definitional, at least provide traits or descriptions which are suggestive of a definition.
12   For connections between 'wisdom of love' and 'the third' see also PJL, 104 and UN, 195, where we see that the introduction of the third is the beginning of philosophy as the wisdom of love.

13 Although the uppercase "Other" usually denotes "*autrui*" (the personal or particular 'Other') and the lowercase 'other' usually denotes "*autre*" (the impersonal or general 'other'), there is no wide agreement as to when to use upper-
or lowercase, since Levinas was not entirely consistent in using these himself.
Thus, I will follow the convention used by most of the contributors to Jeffrey
Bloechl's *The Face of the Other and The Trace of God*. There, they simply "capi-
talize all instances of the word "Other" (whether *autre* or *autrui*). When quoting from translated or secondary literature, however, I will quote exactly as it is
found in the text from which I quote.

14 See also ENP, 123, 27, 30, and 31.

15 The term 'justice' is not used consistently throughout the corpus. In early texts,
such as Totality and Infinity, justice is used synonymously with 'ethical relation'
(see TI, 72). But in later texts, justice becomes associated with terms like 'wisdom' and 'philosophy.' Levinas was aware of this shift in his usage of the term,
as is indicated in when he says, "In *Totality and Infinity* I used the word 'justice'
for ethics, for the relationship between two people. I spoke of 'justice', although
now 'justice' is for me something which is a calculation, which is knowledge,
and which supposes politics; it is inseparable from the political" (PM, 171). I
will be using the term as it was used in the later texts—that is, as a political calculation.

16 This comparison of the Other and the third seems to contradict the incomparable and irreducible nature of the Other. I will address this apparent contradiction in chapters 3 and 4, but I will say at this point that for Levinas, even
though justice removes the distinctions between the Other and the third, it
must do so without completely ignoring the absolute obligation to the Other.
This tension is best expressed when he writes that "justice remains justice only,
in a society where there is no distinction between those close [i.e., the Other]
and those far off [i.e., the third], but in which there also remains the impossibility of passing by the closest" (OB, 159).

17 I address how Levinas resolves this tension in chapters 3 and 4.

18 That these terms are not mutually exclusive is evidenced when Levinas says,
"What shows itself thematically in the synchrony of the said in fact lets itself be
unsaid as a difference of what cannot be assembled, signifying as the one-for-
the-other, from me to the other. The very exhibition of the difference goes
diachronically from the said to the unsaid" (OB, 155). In other words, the 'said'
does not always destroy the 'saying'—when the saying becomes said, it does not
necessarily imply the elimination of the saying. "For thematization, in which
being's essence is conveyed before us, and theory and thought, its contemporaries, do not attest to some fall of the saying. They are motivated by the pre-
original vocation of the saying, by responsibility itself" (OB, 6). I will make this
case at greater length in chapters 3 and 4.

19 See chapters 3 and 4.

20 The term 'love of wisdom' is used primarily when juxtaposed to the phrase 'wisdom of love,' but the term 'anonymous' is used more frequently than love of

wisdom and better describes the quality of wisdom which Levinas critiques. Therefore, 'anonymous wisdom' is the primary term I will use to refer in general to these types of wisdom that are in contrast to the wisdom of love.

21 This passage also serves to show the linkage between these terms: 'being,' 'totality,' 'the State,' 'politics,' 'techniques,' 'work,' and 'weighing.'

22 It would be easy to misinterpret Levinas as saying that all politics, philosophy, and states are to be rejected since they all are necessarily self-serving. This warning, however, implies that it is possible that politics is capable of existing without completely becoming its "own center of gravity."

23 Again, one could mistakenly interpret Levinas to be saying that all justice, politics, and philosophy amounts to this depersonalized, calculating abuse, but this warning implies the possibility for a justice that is *not* purely calculating. This alternative type of justice will be addressed in the next section, "Wisdom of Love."

24 Thomas Hobbes, *Leviathan, Parts One and Two* (New York: Liberal Arts Press, 1958).

25 In the three quotes that follow, I have italicized the terms that I have identified as occurring frequently in close association with 'wisdom.'

26 For other key passages linking these and more terms related to 'wisdom of love' see also OB, 157, 159–60; *DR*, 159, 168; and PP, 142.

27 I will say more in chapter 4 about Levinas's argument that a politics born out of violence has no ultimate limit against violence. But for here, it is sufficient to show the distinction between two views of the origin of justice and politics, and that Levinas is critical of the Hobbesian view.

28 The term 'love' is especially absent in his early work, but even when it shows up with greater frequency in his later works, it is still rare that he uses it without qualification; usually he specifies the way he is using the term, such as "love without concupiscence," "love without reciprocity," or "love of one's neighbor."

29 I will offer three examples of this unconventional terminology. First, when Levinas uses the term 'insatiable desire,' this can easily be mistaken to mean a desire which seeks satiation but never is completely sated. However, he uses the term more technically and actually means a desire which is 'a-satiable.' A second example of possible terminological confusion arises from the fact that one of the terms Levinas used most frequently to refer to this satiable desire was 'need,' and one of the terms most frequently used to refer to the desire that is not satiable is 'metaphysical desire' or sometimes just more simply, 'desire.' One might expect the more commonplace contrast of the terms need and desire whereby the term desire is associated with the baser, erotic love, rather than with the more elevated agapeistic love. A third example of possible terminological misunderstanding arises from the fact that there is a literature (Anders Nygren, Gene Outka, among others) surrounding the contrast between *eros'* and *agape*, and the distinction as it is used in this tradition focuses on the unconditional giving nature of *agape* and the selfish, conditional, receiving

nature of *eros*. Thus when Levinas uses the terms *eros* and *agape* to highlight a satiable/a-satiable distinction rather than a conditional giving/unconditional giving distinction, this is apt to lead those familiar with the latter to mistake Levinas's project as having the same focus. There are many other examples of unconventional, technical uses of terminology that require clarification to help establish the centrality of this satiable/a-satiable distinction, and I will attempt to treat many of these in this chapter.

30 When he uses the term 'insatiable desire,' Levinas does not mean that the desire is incapable of being finally satiated. So a desire that is capable of being temporarily satiated is not described by Levinas as insatiable desire but is a-satiable desire. I will say more about what makes insatiable desire distinct from satiable desire, in the following section on a-satiable desire.

31 Also referring to the capacity for the satiation of need are the terms 'separation,' 'interiority,' 'being at home,' and 'living from.' 'Separation' is what results from this 'enjoyment' of need: "Enjoyment separates by engaging in the contents from which it lives" (TI, 147). But in the ego who is isolated with his engagement with enjoyment is an "imprisoned being, ignorant of its prison" and this illusion that maintains the ignorance "constitutes the separation" (TI, 55). This separation is made possible by 'interiority': "The interiority of enjoyment is separation in itself, is the mode according to which such an event as separation can be produced" (TI, 147). Showing this interconnection of these terms, Levinas writes, "To be separated is to be at home with oneself. But to be at home with oneself . . . is to live from, to enjoy the elemental" (TI, 147). See also the connection to 'being at home' (TI, 143), and enjoyment as interiorization (TI, 142).

32 'Saying' is used in contrast to 'said' which was treated in the first section of this chapter.

33 While *agape* is not frequently used the in his *oeuvre*, it nonetheless makes appearances in his vocabulary. It is usually found paired with *eros* and is juxtaposed in contrast to *eros*. For example, in "Philosophy, Justice and Love," he made the comment, "I don't think that Agape comes from Eros," and, "Eros is definitely not Agape" (113). Furthermore, John Davenport addresses the question of whether it is appropriate to speak of *agape* in reference to Levinas's discussions of love for the Other. He writes that it "will doubtless be protested that Levinas's ethics is meant as a phenomenological metaphysics and is nothing like the sort of theology with which the term '*agape*' is associated." Davenport notes that "Levinas does not focus on constructing an *agape theory* of ethics" but perceptively explains that nonetheless, "it would be difficult to maintain that he constantly invokes the Hebrew categories of the *neighbor* and the *stranger*— with their unmistakable allusion to the love commandments in the Torah—*only* for what they can contribute figuratively to a characterization of transcendence" ("Levinas's Agapeistic Metaphysics of Morals: Absolute Passivity and the Other as Eschatological Hierophany," *Journal of Religious Ethics* 26 (1998): 334;

emphasis in the original). It is with that qualification, therefore, that I will speak of what Levinas has to say about *agape*—Levinas can be brought into conversation with the theological discussion of *agape* a la Nygren, Outka, and others, even though his usage of the term is not identical.

34   For other references in *Entre Nous* connecting 'love without concupiscence' or similar terms with 'responsibility for the Other' or similar terms, see EN, 103, 169, 186, and 216.

35   Plato writes much about the "insatiable desires" (*Republic* 8.544c–564b), which, unchecked, lead to the downfall of states (and souls). It seems noncoincidental that Levinas chooses and repeatedly uses that very term—'insatiable desires'—to describe the highest state of transcendence—one's infinite responsibility for the Other.

36   Levinas does not use the term 'a-satiable,' but I use it here as a term that is interchangeable with Levinas's insatiable desire.

37   Conscience is often used interchangeably with desire.

38   Although it is important to understand the absolute nature of this heteronomy, it is also crucial to note that this heteronomy is not merely to be understood in terms of self-negation. Levinas made this clear when he wrote, "'being for the Other' is not the negation of the I" (TI, 304). This creates an obvious tension between absolute heteronomy and avoiding complete self-negation, and I will address this tension later in this chapter, and more fully in chapters 3 and 4.

39   Similar distinctions between types of freedom can also be found in Augustine's *On Free Choice of the Will* (Augustine, *On Free Choice of the Will,* trans. Thomas Williams [Indianapolis: Hackett, 1993], 57, 68) and Kierkegaard's *Works of Love* (Søren Kierkegaard, *Works of Love: Some Christian Reflections in the Form of Discourses* [New York: Harper, 1962], 52–53).

40   The relationship between these two types of freedom will be addressed more fully in subsequent chapters.

41   See TI, 254; OB, 31, 88, 102, 122–23, 132, 150, 179, and 194 for just a few of the many examples of the use of this term.

42   To emphasize further the Other-initiated quality of this freedom, Levinas draws attention to the fact that the 'me voici' is in the accusative case (OB, 142, 146, 149).

Chapter 3

1   I will refer to the former as a nonreductionist view while the latter will be called a reductionist view.

2   While 'need' and 'desire' are the predominant terms used in the earlier texts, the corresponding terms of 'concupiscence' and 'neighbor-love' are used more frequently in the later texts. As I have shown, there is a strong connection between these sets of terms, and since most of Levinas's most mature thought on the issues of reductionism come in the later texts, I will refer to the set of terms used most frequently there—that is, concupiscence (relating to need and satiable desire) and neighbor-love (relating to a-satiable desire).

3 Jeffery Bloechl, "How Best to Keep a Secret? On Love and Respect in Levinas's 'Phenomenology of Eros'," *Man and World* 29 (1996): 1, 12.

4 Bloechl, "How Best to Keep a Secret?" 15.

5 Levinas writes that "with Freud, sexuality is approached on the human plane, it is reduced to the level of the search for pleasure, without . . . the irreducible categories it brings into play even suspected" (TI, 276).

6 I use the term consensus not as a synonym with unanimity, since obviously there is at least one who disagrees (Bloechl, "How Best to Keep a Secret?"); rather, I use consensus in the Quaker sense of the term, meaning an overall sense of agreement. But the fact that there is this level of agreement should be enjoyed, because on most of the issues, which I will subsequently be addressing, there is not only a wide variety of views, but a significant difference between some of the varying opinions. Hopefully, this work can at least bring some clarity as to why there are these differences, even if it may not help move us closer to consensus on these matters of interpretation.

7 For discussion of the gift, see the following: Marcel Mauss, *The Gift: Forms and Functions of Exchange in Archaic Societies* (Glencoe, Ill.: Free Press, 1954); Jacques Derrida, *The Gift of Death, Religion and Postmodernism* (Chicago: University of Chicago Press, 1995); Alan D. Schrift, *The Logic of the Gift: Toward an Ethic of Generosity* (New York: Routledge, 1997); John D. Caputo, *The Prayers and Tears of Jacques Derrida: Religion without Religion,* Indiana Series in the Philosophy of Religion (Bloomington: Indiana University Press, 1997); John D. Caputo, *Deconstruction in a Nutshell: A Conversation with Jacques Derrida,* Perspectives in Continental Philosophy (New York: Fordham University Press, 1997); John Milbank, "The Ethics of Self-Sacrifice," *First Things* 91 (1999); John D. Caputo and Michael J. Scanlon, eds., *God, the Gift, and Postmodernism,* The Indiana Series in the Philosophy of Religion (Bloomington: Indiana University Press, 1999); Robyn Horner, *Rethinking God as Gift: Marion, Derrida and the Limits of Phenomenology,* Perspectives in Continental Philosophy (New York: Fordham University Press, 2001).

8 Jacques Derrida, *Given Time: I. Counterfeit Money,* trans. Peggy Kamuf (Chicago: University of Chicago Press, 1991), 82.

9 Even if not one common language, it is still true "in a few familiar languages" he qualifies later. Derrida, *Given Time,* 11, 12.

10 Derrida, *Given Time,* 12.

11 When Caputo discusses Levinas's view on what I have called neighbor-love, some of the terms he employs to capture this include: 'absolute altruism,' 'infinite alterity,' and 'obligation' (e.g., see John D. Caputo, *Against Ethics: Contributions to a Poetics of Obligation with Constant Reference to Deconstruction,* Studies in Continental Thought [Bloomington: Indiana University Press, 1993], 80, 82, and 126 respectively).

12 Caputo, *Against Ethics,* 83.

13 John D. Caputo, "Apostles of the Impossible," in *God, the Gift, and Postmodernism,* ed. Caputo and Scanlon, 185–86.

14 Caputo, *Against Ethics*, 83.

15 Caputo, *Against Ethics*, 79, 82. Caputo likes Levinas's dream, though, and also says that Levinas's absolute obligation is "as it stands in Levinas, the dream of virgin lands and arctic snows" (82).

16 Stephen H. Webb, "The Rhetoric of Ethics as Excess: A Christian Theological Response to Emmanuel Levinas," *Modern Theology* 15, no. 1 (1999): 4.

17 Richard Kearney, "On the Gift," in *God, the Gift, and Postmodernism*, ed. Caputo and Scanlon, 59.

18 Richard Kearney, "Desire of God," in *God, the Gift, and Postmodernism*, ed. Caputo and Scanlon, 121. Kearney shows his alignment with Caputo's interpretation, quoting his essay, John D. Caputo, "Hyperbolic Justice," in his *Demythologizing Heidegger*, Indiana Series in Philosophy of Religion (Bloomington: Indiana University Press, 1993), 200–201.

19 Horner, *Rethinking God as Gift*, 69.

20 Paul Ricoeur, *Oneself as Another*, trans. Kathleen Blamey (Chicago: University of Chicago Press, 1992), 336–41, 338, 337.

21 Ricoeur, *Oneself as Another*, 181–94.

22 I used to think that an Aristotelian understanding of self-love was just the corrective that Levinas needed (and I argued for this in a paper I presented three years ago at the Fordham Graduate Philosophical Symposium, May 2001). *Philia*, after all, seems to be the perfect 'third way' between *eros* and *agape*. However, while I still think that some elements of Aristotelian mutuality are consistent with Levinas (as I shall discuss later in this chapter), I can no longer see how viewing the self as the initiator of obligation could be compatible with Levinas's philosophy, since the opposite is one of his core views.

23 Ricoeur, *Oneself as Another*, 188–89.

24 Richard A. Cohen, "Moral Selfhood: A Levinasian Response to Ricoeur on Levinas," in *Ricoeur as Another*, ed. Cohen and Marsh, 129. Cohen observes that it is because he "misunderstands the level of significance of the alterity of the other in Levinas, that Ricoeur misunderstands, in addition, the passivity of the self that responds to alterity. The Levinasian self is not so separate as to be inviolate, simply passive, or as Ricoeur would have it, the (im)possible object of violence and war." Rather, the passivity refers to "the moral self's irreplacability" (134).

25 Luce Irigaray, "The Fecundity of the Caress: A Reading of Levinas, Totality and Infinity, 'Phenomenology of Eros'," in his *An Ethics of Sexual Difference* (Ithaca: Cornell University Press, 1993), 178.

26 Luce Irigaray, "Questions to Emmanuel Levinas: On the Divinity of Love," in *Re-Reading Levinas*, ed. Robert Bernasconi and Simon Critchley (Indianapolis: Indiana University Press, 1991).

27 Irigaray, "Questions to Emmanuel Levinas," 115.

28 Tina Chanter, *Ethics of Eros: Irigaray's Re-Writing of the Philosophers* (New York: Routledge, 1995), 308 n. 62, 194. (The quote following the ellipsis is Chanter's use of Levinas.)

29 Chanter, *Ethics of Eros*, 203, 222.

30 Stella Sandford, *The Metaphysics of Love: Gender and Transcendence in Levinas* (New Brunswick, N.J.: Athlone Press, 2000), 51.

31 Sandford, *Metaphysics of Love*, 140.

32 Claire Elise Katz, "For Love Is as Strong as Death," *Philosophy Today* 45, no. 5 (2001): 126.

33 Katz, "For Love Is as Strong as Death," 127.

34 Katz, "For Love Is as Strong as Death," 126.

35 See also Claire Elise Katz, *Levinas, Judaism, and the Feminine: The Silent Footsteps of Rebecca*, Indiana Series in the Philosophy of Religion (Bloomington: Indiana University Press, 2003).

36 Kearney, "On the Gift," 60.

37 Derrida, *Given Time*, 11.

38 In a response to a paper I gave on the topic of Derrida's gift, John Drummond said he thought that the gift, as described by Derrida, was simply a poor and incomplete phenomenological analysis of giving. (May 2001).

39 Milbank, "The Ethics of Self-Sacrifice."

40 For example, in *Thus Spoke Zarathustra*, we find that neighbor love not only lacks authenticity, but it arises out of distorted self-love: "[Y]our love of the neighbor is your bad love of yourselves. You flee to your neighbor from yourselves and would like to make a virtue out of that: but I see through your 'selflessness'" (Friedrich Wilhelm Nietzsche, *Thus Spoke Zarathustra: A Book for All and None*, trans. Walter Kaufmann [New York: Viking Press, 1966], 60).

41 As examples of the many who have taken compatibilist positions (though varying in several different ways) see the following: Gene H. Outka, *Agape: An Ethical Analysis*, Yale Publications in Religion (New Haven: Yale University Press, 1972); Oliver O'Donovan, *The Problem of Self-Love in St. Augustine* (New Haven: Yale University Press, 1980); Vincent Brümmer, *The Model of Love: A Study in Philosophical Theology* (New York: Cambridge University Press, 1993).

42 For example, I have explained that Levinas could not have held views of reciprocity urged upon him by Ricoeur. In that sense, I am asking, could Levinas have been a compatibilist?

43 Adriaan Theodoor Peperzak, *To the Other*, Purdue University Series in the History of Philosophy (West Lafayette, Ind.: Purdue University Press, 1993), 133.

44 Peperzak, *To the Other*, 193.

45 Peperzak, *To the Other*, 120, 133.

46 Adriaan Theodoor Peperzak, *Beyond: The Philosophy of Emmanuel Levinas*, Northwestern University Studies in Phenomenology and Existential Philosophy (Evanston, Ill.: Northwestern University Press, 1997), 168, 169 n. 5.

47 Merold Westphal, "Commanded Love and Divine Transcendence in Levinas and Kierkegaard," in *The Face of the Other and the Trace of God*, ed. Bloechl, 217.

48 Westphal, "Commanded Love and Divine Transcendence," 216, 218. Westphal concludes the essay quoting another Jewish philosopher—Spinoza—who said that "all things excellent are as difficult as they are rare" (218).

49 Westphal, "Commanded Love and Divine Transcendence," 217.

50 Ricoeur also thought Levinas *should* be a compatibilist, but Olthuis and Davenport, unlike Ricoeur, provide a view of compatibilism which *could* be embraced by Levinas.

51 Davenport, "Levinas's Agapeistic Metaphysics of Morals," 339, 342.

52 James H. Olthuis, *Knowing Other-Wise: Philosophy at the Threshold of Spirituality*, Perspectives in Continental Philosophy (New York: Fordham University Press, 1997), 143, 132, 150.

53 Olthuis, *Knowing Other-Wise*, 248. For a classic example of the incompatibilist position of *agape* and *eros* (which is in contrast to the various theological compatibilist views cited in n. 41 of this chapter), see Anders Nygren, *Agape and Eros* (Chicago: University of Chicago Press, 1982).

54 Among those who think Levinas could be a compatibilist, I would also include Westphal and Peperzak, who not only interpret Levinas as a compatibilist, but view this as consistent with the rest of his thought—at least, I have not read either of them making claims to the contrary.

55 See chapter 2, where I show Levinas's definition of the third. I will also be showing in detail in chapter 4 how the role of the third is often ignored and leads to misinterpretations of Levinas.

56 Peperzak, *Beyond*, 169 n. 5.

57 Peperzak, *To the Other*, 230.

58 The discussions by Nygren and his interlocutors, like the discussions of Derrida and his interlocutors, have focused on the notion of giving. And as is made especially clear by Derrida and those engaging him, this discussion often narrows the focus even further to the gift itself. It becomes like a game of tennis where the only way to achieve neighbor-love is to give the tennis ball to the other person without receiving it back. The focus is on the tennis ball. Levinas does not share this focus, however, since his discussion of neighbor-love is focused not on the thing given or received in return, but on the desire. While Derrida watches to see if any *thing* gets given back, Levinas watches for the *desire* of the Other. We see this by his frequent use of terms such as 'metaphysical desire' and 'insatiable desire' to describe neighbor-love, but it is clear in other ways as well.

59 O. Henry, "The Gift of the Magi," in *The Complete Works of O. Henry* (Garden City, N.Y.: Doubleday, 1953). The fact that their sacrifices made their gifts useless to each other was not viewed as foolishness, but the narrator says that "of all who give gifts these two were the wisest" (11).

60 In other words, seeking a pure conscience leads us into a problem raised by Nietzsche, which is expressed in the following: "It is those farther away who must pay for your love of your neighbor; and even if five of you are together, there is always a sixth who must die" (*Thus Spoke Zarathustra*, 61).

61 In chapter 5, I will be treating some actual examples in order to show this, but I will defer argument for this point at present.

62 Tamra Wright, Peter Hughes, and Alison Ainley, "The Paradox of Morality," in *Provocation of Levinas*, ed. Robert Bernasconi and David Wood (New York: Routledge, 1988), 176.

Chapter 4

1   See chapter 2 of this book.
2   This claim is defended throughout the corpus, but can be seen most explicitly in the following: "Is Ontology Fundamental?" (1996), Section I.A.4 "Metaphysics Precedes Ontology," in *Totality and Infinity* (1969), Section III.B "Ethics and the Face," in *Totality and Infinity* (1969), and "Ethics as First Philosophy," in *The Levinas Reader* (1989).
3   Unless otherwise noted, all emphases within the quotes cited in this chapter are mine.
4   These various interpretations will be treated in §4 of this chapter.
5   Peperzak, *To the Other*, 34.
6   Luc Bouckaert, "Ontology and Ethics: Reflections on Levinas's Critique of Heidegger," *International Philosophical Quarterly* 10 (1970): 418, 410.
7   Theodorus de Boer, *The Rationality of Transcendence: Studies in the Philosophy of Emmanuel Levinas,* Amsterdam Studies in Jewish Thought 4 (Amsterdam: J. C. Gieben, 1997), 28.
8   For an expansion of this point, see the currently unpublished paper I presented last May (2006) at the North American Levinas Society Conference entitled, "Levinas and the Birth of the Political: Maieutics or Maternity? or A Prolegomena to any Future Politics." In response to the concern about Levinas and a lack of any concrete ethical or political theory, I would not try to argue that he does provide an ethics or a politics, if by that we mean first-order ethical or political philosophy. But the fact that he does not provide a concrete ethic or politic does not mean that his thinking precludes or is antithetical to one. How might we be helped if instead of looking to Levinas for a political schematic, we instead saw him as providing a "prolegomena to any future politics"?
9   Boer, *Rationality of Transcendence*, 26, 28.
10 Boer, *Rationality of Transcendence*, 28.
11 Boer, *Rationality of Transcendence*, 31.
12 Ricoeur, *Oneself as Another*, 189.
13 He also refers to Gyges in "Truth of Disclosure and Truth of Testimony," 104, 105, and 146.
14 See *Republic* 359d–360b and 612b. See also Herodotus, I.8ff.
15 This "determination of the other by the same, without the same being determined by the other" is how Levinas defines 'representation' (TI, 170) further revealing the cognitive aspect of Gyges' "seeing without being seen."
16 The term 'nonrecognized' here not only alludes to the invisibility of Gyges but it also carries cognitive connotations pertaining to being free from the conceptual categories of others.

17 The ethical implication is that by becoming an unknown knower, one isolates himself such that he is separated from the accusation of the Other.

18 To 'totalize,' as Levinas uses the term, is to reduce the Other to something less than the Other and to think that this reduction has captured all of the Other.

19 Derrida, "Violence and Metaphysics," 146.

20 Derrida, "Violence and Metaphysics," 152.

21 Derrida, "Violence and Metaphysics," 116, 117.

22 See discussion under the subheading "The Gyges Test" of this chapter, explaining how Levinas also uses 'light' in the Gyges myth to represent 'comprehension of being.'

23 Derrida, "Violence and Metaphysics," 117; emphasis in the original.

24 I am not necessarily defending the claim that Llewelyn holds this view, but these comments by him at least represent what a defender of this view might say.

25 John Llewelyn, "Levinas, Derrida and Others Vis-a-Vis," in The Provocation of Levinas Rethinking the Other, Warwick Studies in Philosophy and Literature (London/New York: Routledge, 1988), 154; my emphasis.

26 Derrida, in defending the lesser violence, says that the less violent "discourse chooses itself violently in opposition to nothingness or pure non-sense, and, in philosophy, against nihilism" ("Violence and Metaphysics," 130).

27 M. Jamie Ferreira, "'Total Altruism' in Levinas's 'Ethics of the Welcome'," Journal of Religious Ethics 29, no. 3 (2001): 443–470.

28 Ferreira, "'Total Altruism'," 464.

29 For further discussion of the third, see Peperzak, To the Other, 167–84.

30 Peter Atterton, "Levinas and the Language of Peace: A Response to Derrida," Philosophy Today 36, no. 1/4 (1992): 59–70.

31 See Derrida, "Violence and Metaphysics."

32 Atterton, "Levinas and the Language of Peace," 68; emphasis in original.

33 See the following: Peperzak, To the Other, 167–84. Robert Gibbs, Why Ethics? Signs of Responsibilities (Princeton: Princeton University Press, 2000), 17, 134–37; William Paul Simmons, "The Third: Levinas's Theoretical Move from an-Archical Ethics to the Realm of Justice and Politics," Philosophy and Social Criticism 25, no. 6 (1999): 92–100; Atterton, "Levinas and the Language of Peace."

34 Ferreira, "'Total Altruism'," 455; my emphasis.

35 Burggraeve, Wisdom of Love in the Service of Love, 140.

36 For more on the difference between Levinas and Buber, see TI, 68–69; OB, 13; AT, 57, 93, and 94.

37 Levinas wrote, "If I am alone with the other, I owe him everything; but there is someone else" by which he meant, the third is always present—I am never alone with the Other. See Emmanuel Levinas, Ethics and Infinity: Conversations with Philippe Nemo, ed. Richard A. Cohen (Pittsburgh: Duquesne University Press, 1985), 90.

38 Ferreira "'Total Altruism'," 466, 467; my emphasis.

39 Simmons, "The Third," 83, 90, 92; my emphasis.

40 See also TI, 101, where he says that "freedom does not have the last word."

41 I choose this term because 'inversion' indicates that there is a change in hierarchical priority, but 'pacific' indicates that this inversion is not a mere reversal, since the new hierarchy is not the same qualitatively as what it is replacing. I will say more about this later, but the term pacific points to the peaceful quality of this hierarchy, and as mentioned earlier, for Levinas, 'peace' is much more than the mere absence of violence. I hope to reflect each of these qualities in the term 'pacific inversion of priority.' For sake of brevity, I will sometimes refer to this as 'pacific priority' or 'inversion priority.'

42 The term also is found in later writing such as in his essay "Peace and Proximity" which is found in *Alterity and Transcendence*.

43 Atterton, "Levinas and the Language of Peace," 67, 68.

44 Atterton, "Levinas and the Language of Peace," 60; my emphasis.

45 Levinas uses 'power' and 'force' synonymously, and I will do so as well.

46 Ricoeur, *Oneself as Another*, 189.

47 Besides not necessarily having the power to enforce the authority, it should be noted that when I say the Other has authority over me, I do not mean that whatever the Other says for me to do is authoritative. The face and voice of the Other is where I encounter the traces of this authority, but if the Other for whom I am responsible tells me to go kill someone, this is not the authority of which Levinas is speaking. The Other for whom I am responsible might even say to me "Kill me," and obeying the trace of the authority in that Other would mean doing precisely the opposite of what he verbally demanded me to do.

48 Emmanuel Levinas, "Emmanuel Levinas," in *French Philosophers in Conversation*, ed. Raoul Mortley (New York: Routledge, 1991), 15, 16.

49 It should be noted that being elected by the Good is equivalent to being commanded by this authority, but here as discussed earlier, this election can be resisted, even though it cannot be changed. One can either disobey or obey this command—one can either refuse or welcome this Good.

Chapter 5

1 This is found in the collection of essays gathered and published under the title *Alterity and Transcendence*.

2 Of course, it only takes one counterexample to disprove an absolute, and many such as Karl Popper have challenged the possibility of proving any positive claim, arguing instead that we can only prove the falsification of a thesis. Thus I make two clarifications. First, I am not seeking to prove the absolute power of the Other, as I have already mentioned. Secondly, I am not seeking to prove absolutely the absolute authority of the Other. But I will be providing evidence and then offering an argument by inference to the best explanation.

3   The first three chapters have primarily been an argument for a particular interpretation of Levinas—namely, that Levinas thinks that wisdom of love is possible, and that it is indeed possible. Furthermore, I have been arguing that it is
significantly different from other types of wisdom. The major objection I am
trying to answer in this chapter is to what degree this wisdom of love, if possible, is truly different from other forms of wisdom. Since Levinas did not provide much in the way of practical applications of this ethical metaphysics, I will
be turning to other sources, such as the examples already cited. I am not arguing that this is exactly what Levinas had in mind, but I think it is compatible,
for the most part, with his philosophy, and I also think that this goes some distance in showing that this view produces a wisdom that is truly different than,
say, a Hobbesian account.

4   There are many genocides from which I could choose, and within each genocide, there are many stories that could be told, many studies conducted. For the
sake of continuity and for the sake of going into depth in these accounts, I will
be focusing primarily on two parallel groups of people, the townspeople of Le
Chambon, and the Nazi Doctors of Auschwitz, who responded to the authority of the Other in different ways.

5   Philip Hallie, *Lest Innocent Blood Be Shed* (New York: Harper Perennial, 1994),
120, 124; emphasis in original.

6   Hallie, *Lest Innocent Blood Be Shed*, 274, 127, 293; emphasis in original.

7   Hannah Arendt, *Eichmann in Jerusalem: A Report on the Banality of Evil*, rev.
and enl. ed. (New York: Viking Press, 1964).

8   Robert Jay Lifton, *The Nazi Doctors: Medical Killing and the Psychology of
Genocide* (New York: Basic Books, 1986), 5, 423.

9   Lifton, *Nazi Doctors*, 454, 159.

10   Lifton, *Nazi Doctors*, 436, 446; my emphasis.

11   Lifton, *Nazi Doctors*, 162.

12   See also Finkielkraut, *Wisdom of Love*. His description of the ways in which
Nazis used physical invisibility (108–13) reinforces this role of physical invisibility in enabling violence to the Other.

13   Lifton, *Nazi Doctors*, 17, 439, 441.

14   Lifton, *Nazi Doctors*, 445, 77.

15   Lifton, *Nazi Doctors*, 421; emphasis in the original.

16   Lifton, *Nazi Doctors*, 451.

17   Lifton, *Nazi Doctors*, 444; my emphasis.

18   Hallie, *Lest Innocent Blood Be Shed*, xxi, 132.

19   Hallie, *Lest Innocent Blood Be Shed*, 287.

20   Hallie, *Lest Innocent Blood Be Shed*, 107.

21   Lifton, *Nazi Doctors*, 464, 503, 499.

22   See §3 of chapter 4.

23   Although I will be focusing on the visual aspects of Gyges' secret—namely
invisibility and visibility—this also has implications for hearing and speaking.
"Gyges plays a double game . . . speaking to 'others' and evading speech" (TI,

173). That is, what is said about becoming invisible to the Other while seeing the Other has parallels in speech, such that Gyges might speak demands to the Other while remaining deaf to the commands that come from the Other. The auditory parallel to vision as it applies to the face of the Other is addressed in many places including hearing the 'call' or 'summons' of the Other (OB, 114), the contrast of 'speaking' and 'listening' (TI, 296), the 'resonance' or 'resounding' of the Other (OB, 38–41), and even the 'listening eye' (OB, 30, 37, 38).

24   Herodotus and Carter, *Here Are Set Forth*, 1:8ff.

25   This was already alluded to in chapter 3, and is found in the *Republic* 359d–360b and 612b.

26   See chapter 3 for a description of the Gyges test.

27   Frederick Charles Copleston, *A History of Philosophy* (Garden City, N.Y.: Doubleday, 1993), 1:405.

28   Hallie, *Lest Innocent Blood Be Shed*, 128; my emphasis.

29   Herodotus and Carter, *Here Are Set Forth*, 4.

30   The text reads: "So Gyges, not being able to do otherwise, consented" (Herodotus and Carter, *Here Are Set Forth*, 4). Of course it is not that he was unable to do otherwise, but he was unable to do otherwise without putting his own safety and position in jeopardy.

31   Herodotus and Carter, *Here Are Set Forth*, 5.

32   *Republic* 359a–360b.

33   Although I do not have space to sufficiently treat this point, it would be worth exploring at some future occasion the implications of the absence of any deductive proof for one's ethical obligation to the Other from the fact of one's autonomous experience. One might defend the position that the absence of such a proof does not negate the fact that I am responsible for the Other more than myself; it could be argued, instead, that my responsibility for the Other is so fundamentally basic to who I am that the inability to derive this fact from my autonomous experience weighs against the validity of viewing my autonomous experience as properly basic. In the same way that one could not derive water from hydrogen alone, so one could argue that it is impossible to derive ethical responsibility from an autonomous individual. The absence of proof is not evidence that water does not exist. Rather, the existence of water, combined with the inability to derive it from hydrogen alone, is evidence for the insufficiency of hydrogen. Likewise, it could be argued, the inability to derive ethical responsibility for the Other from autonomous experience is evidence for the insufficiency of autonomous experience.

34   Hallie, *Lest Innocent Blood Be Shed*, 286, 274; emphasis in the original.

35   Hallie, *Lest Innocent Blood Be Shed*, xviii, 287.

36   Merold Westphal, "Levinas and the Immediacy of the Face," *Faith and Philosophy* 10, no. 4 (1993): 499.

37   Derrida, "Violence and Metaphysics," 82.

38   See "Breaking the Secret by Opposing Gyges?" in this chapter.

39   Hallie, *Lest Innocent Blood Be Shed*, 10, 101, 8, 102.

40   He was only half Jewish.

41   One could say that there is much overlap between 'prophecy,' 'teaching,' and 'testimony' but that these are just shifting terms for very similar ideas. I would say that they are more similar than they are different, but I will treat each of them, because even if they were entirely synonymous, the different treatments in the different texts reveal more collectively than any one in isolation.

42   Proverbs 9:8b. The Holy Bible: New Revised Standard Version, Containing the Old and New Testaments (Nashville: Thomas Nelson Publishers, 1989).

43   Section 7, that is, on 'Forms of Speaking with Wisdom of Love.'

44   Abraham said "Here I am" (Gen 22:1, 22:11); Jacob said, "Here I am" (Gen 31:11, 46:2); Moses said, "Here I am" (Exod 3:4); Samuel said, "Here I am" (1 Sam 3:4); and Isaiah said, "Here am I" (Isa 6:8, 8:18, 58:9).

45   Hallie, Lest Innocent Blood Be Shed, 128; my emphasis.

46   He also refers to the "Here I am" as the "secret of sociality" in OT, 149 and in OUJ, 228.

47   We see elsewhere the close association by Levinas of 'testimony' and 'revelation.' For example, Levinas writes that "ethical testimony is a revelation which is not a knowledge" (GT, 108).

48   These, of course, were the words spoken by Magda Trocmé to the Jewish refugee. Hallie, Lest Innocent Blood Be Shed, 287.

Chapter 6

1   For example, see US, NC, PP.

2   Zygmunt Bauman, Globalization: The Human Consequences, European Perspectives (New York: Columbia University Press, 1998), 48.

3   Perhaps this is why, in Schindler's List, the audience is helped to focus on one girl by her wearing a red coat in an otherwise black-and-white film. We might be able to hide from several thousand faces being mistreated, but it is much more difficult to remain invisible and concealed when we see one single face as unique. This one girl, like Anne Frank, can do more to break the secret of Gyges than a page full of statistics of thousands shot and millions gassed.

4   The material quoted was paraphrased by the interviewer and was in reference to Vasiliæi Semenovich Grossman, Life and Fate: A Novel (London: Collins Harvill, 1985).

5   John J. Davenport, "Time and Responsibility," paper presented at the All Souls Unitarian Universalist Church, New York, January 2002. Emphasis in the original.

6   See n. 23 in chapter 5 of this book, where I cite many texts where Levinas speaks of 'hearing' the Other.

7   Nietzsche, Thus Spoke Zarathustra, 61.

8   Consider, for example, the practices of 'Agros,' an organization that has been revitalizing areas of Central America by helping to establish sustainable villages in areas previously demolished by internal warfare. They have been very suc-

cessful in their work, but only accept donations of funds if those funds are accompanied with the donor's actual, face-to-face involvement and an extended commitment to a single group of people. They have found that the success of the development depends on this face-to-face interaction, and that anonymous donations from afar are counter productive. Responding to such a need by making a long-term, physical presence with a small group of people is one way in which a call can be received from afar, but answered by becoming a neighbor in physical proximity.

9   Hallie, *Lest Innocent Blood Be Shed*, 113.

10 Hallie, *Lest Innocent Blood Be Shed*, 128, 8, 9.

11 Richard J. Foster, *Celebration of Discipline: The Path to Spiritual Growth*, (San Francisco: Harper & Row, 1978), 17.

12 This project was called Operation T4, and in August of 1941 Hitler gave the order to end or at least stall the operation. Lifton, *Nazi Doctors*, 95.

13 One could find further theoretical support for this claim by drawing upon De Tocqueville's analysis of 'mediating institutions.' See Alexis de Tocqueville and Stephen D. Grant, *Democracy in America* (Indianapolis: Hackett, 2000).

14 Matthew 18:20 NRSV.

15 Wendell Berry, *Jayber Crow* (Washington, D.C.: Counterpoint, 2000), 143.

Conclusion

1   Admittedly, the type of testimony Levinas spoke of and which I addressed is the testimony of action—of being for the Other. But this form of testimony seems appropriate here, nonetheless.

2   DayDay's given name is Emmanuel.

Bibliography

"40, Mars Hill." *On Globalization* 40 (1999).

Adams, Robert Merrihew. "Pure Love." *Journal of Religious Ethics* 8, no. 1 (1980): 83–99.

———. *Finite and Infinite Goods: A Framework for Ethics.* New York: Oxford University Press, 1999.

Arendt, Hannah. *Eichmann in Jerusalem: A Report on the Banality of Evil.* Rev. and enl. ed. New York: Viking Press, 1964.

Atterton, Peter. "Levinas and the Language of Peace: A Response to Derrida." *Philosophy Today* 36, no. 1/4 (1992): 59–70.

Augustine. *On Free Choice of the Will.* Translated by Thomas Williams. Indianapolis: Hackett, 1993.

Bauman, Zygmunt. *Globalization: The Human Consequences.* European Perspectives. Cambridge: Polity Press, 1998.

Berlin, Isaiah. *The Hedgehog and the Fox: An Essay on Tolstoy's View of History.* New York: Simon & Schuster, 1953.

Bernstein, Richard J. *The New Constellation: The Ethical-Political Horizons of Modernity/Postmodernity.* Cambridge, Mass.: MIT Press, 1992.

Berry, Wendell. *Jayber Crow.* Washington, D.C.: Counterpoint, 2000.

Bloechl, Jeffrey, ed. *The Face of the Other and the Trace of God: Essays on the Philosophy of Emmanuel Levinas.* New York: Fordham University Press, 2000.

———. "How Best to Keep a Secret? On Love and Respect in Levinas's 'Phenomenology of Eros'." *Man and World* 29 (1996): 1–17.

Boer, Theodorus de. *The Rationality of Transcendence: Studies in the Philosophy of Emmanuel Levinas.* Amsterdam Studies in Jewish Thought 4. Amsterdam: J. C. Gieben, 1997.

Bouckaert, Luc. "Ontology and Ethics: Reflections on Levinas's Critique of Heidegger." *International Philosophical Quarterly* 10 (1970): 402–19.

Bourgeois, Patrick L. "Ricoeur and Levinas: Solicitude in Reciprocity and Solitude in Existence." In Cohen and Marsh, *Ricoeur as Another*, 109–26.

Brümmer, Vincent. *The Model of Love: A Study in Philosophical Theology.* New York: Cambridge University Press, 1993.

Burggraeve, Roger. *The Wisdom of Love in the Service of Love: Emmanuel Levinas on Justice, Peace, and Human Rights.* Translated by Jeffrey Bloechl. Milwaukee: Marquette University Press, 2002.

Caputo, John D. *Against Ethics: Contributions to a Poetics of Obligation with Constant Reference to Deconstruction.* Studies in Continental Thought. Bloomington: Indiana University Press, 1993.

———. "Apostles of the Impossible." In Caputo and Scanlon, *God, the Gift, and Postmodernism*, 185–228.

———. *Deconstruction in a Nutshell: A Conversation with Jacques Derrida.* Perspectives in Continental Philosophy. New York: Fordham University Press, 1997.

———. "Hyperbolic Justice." Pages 186–208 in *Demythologizing Heidegger,* edited by John D. Caputo. Indiana Series in the Philosophy of Religion. Bloomington: Indiana University Press, 1993.

———. *The Prayers and Tears of Jacques Derrida: Religion without Religion.* Indiana Series in the Philosophy of Religion. Bloomington: Indiana University Press, 1997.

Caputo, John D., and Michael J. Scanlon, eds. *God, the Gift, and Postmodernism.* Indiana Series in the Philosophy of Religion. Bloomington: Indiana University Press, 1999.

Chanter, Tina. *Ethics of Eros: Irigaray's Re-Writing of the Philosophers.* New York: Routledge, 1995.

Coady, C. A. J. *Testimony: A Philosophical Study.* New York: Clarendon, 1992.

Cohen, Richard. "Humanism and Anti-Humanism: Levinas, Cassirer and Heidegger." Introduction to *Humanism of the Other.* Translated by Nidra Poller. Champaign: University of Illinois Press, 2003.

Cohen, Richard A. *Ethics, Exegesis, and Philosophy: Interpretation after Levinas.* Cambridge: Cambridge University Press, 2001.

———. *Face to Face with Levinas.* SUNY Series in Philosophy. Albany: State University of New York Press, 1986.

———. "Moral Selfhood: A Levinasian Response to Ricoeur on Levinas." Pages 127–60 in Cohen and Marsh, *Ricoeur as Another.*

Cohen, Richard A., and James L. Marsh, eds. *Ricoeur as Another: The Ethics of Subjectivity.* Albany: State University of New York Press, 2002.

Copleston, Frederick Charles. *A History of Philosophy.* 9 vols. Garden City, N.Y.: Doubleday, 1993.

Critchley, Simon, and Robert Bernasconi. *The Cambridge Companion to Levinas.* Cambridge: Cambridge University Press, 2002.

Davenport, John J. "Levinas's Agapeistic Metaphysics of Morals: Absolute Passivity and the Other as Eschatological Hierophany." *Journal of Religious Ethics* 26 (1998): 331–66.

———. "Time and Responsibility." Paper presented at the All Souls Unitarian Universalist Church, New York, January 2002.

Davis, Colin. *Levinas: An Introduction.* Notre Dame, Ind.: University of Notre Dame Press, 1996.

Derrida, Jacques. *Given Time: I. Counterfeit Money.* Translated by Peggy Kamuf. Chicago: University of Chicago Press, 1991.

———. *The Gift of Death, Religion and Postmodernism.* Translated by David Wills. Chicago: University of Chicago Press, 1995.

———. "Violence and Metaphysics: An Essay on the Thought of Emmanuel Levinas." Pages 79–168 in *Writing and Difference*, edited by Alan Bass. Chicago: University of Chicago Press, 1978.

Dudiak, Jeffrey. "Again Ethics: A Levinasian Reading of Caputo Reading Levinas." Pages 172–213 in *Knowing Other-Wise: Philosophy at the Threshold of Spirituality*, edited by James H. Olthuis. New York: Fordham University Press, 1997.

———. *The Intrigue of Ethics: A Reading of the Idea of Discourse in the Thought of Emmanuel Levinas.* Perspectives in Continental Philosophy 18. New York: Fordham University Press, 2001.

Ferreira, M. Jamie. "'Total Altruism' in Levinas's 'Ethics of the Welcome'." *Journal of Religious Ethics* 29, no. 3 (2001): 443–70.

Finkielkraut, Alain. *The Wisdom of Love.* Vol. 20, *Texts and Contexts.* Lincoln: University of Nebraska Press, 1997.

Foster, Richard J. *Celebration of Discipline: The Path to Spiritual Growth.* San Francisco: Harper & Row, 1978.

Gibbs, Robert. "Review of *Ethics, Exegesis, and Philosophy: Interpretation after Levinas* by Richard Cohen." *Notre Dame Philosophical Reviews* (2002).

———. *Why Ethics?: Signs of Responsibilities.* Princeton: Princeton University Press, 2000.

Gordon, Neve. "Ethics as Reciprocity: An Analysis of Levinas's Reading of Buber." *International Studies in Philosophy* 31, no. 2 (1999): 91–109..

Grene, Marjorie. *The Knower and the Known.* Berkeley: University of California Press, 1984.

Grossman, Vasiliæi Semenovich. *Life and Fate: A Novel.* London: Collins Harvill, 1985.

Hadot, Pierre, and Arnold Ira Davidson. *Philosophy as a Way of Life: Spiritual Exercises from Socrates to Foucault.* New York: Blackwell, 1995.

Hallie, Philip. *Lest Innocent Blood Be Shed.* New York: Harper Perennial, 1994.

Hand, Sean. *The Levinas Reader.* Cambridge: Blackwell, 1989.

Hart, Hendrik. *Conceptual Understanding and Knowing Other-Wise: Reflections on Rationality and Spirituality in Philosophy.* New York: Fordham University Press, 1997.

Henry, O. "The Gift of the Magi." Pages 7–11 in *The Complete Works of O. Henry*. Garden City, N.Y.: Doubleday, 1953.

Herodotus. *Here Are Set Forth the Histories of Herodotus of Halicarnassus; That Men's Actions May Not in Time Be Forgotten nor Things Great and Wonderful, Accomplished Whether by Greeks or Barbarians, Go without Report, nor, Especially, the Cause of the Wars between One and the Other*. Ed. Harry Graham Carter. New York: Heritage Press, 1959.

Hobbes, Thomas. *Leviathan, Parts One and Two*. New York: Liberal Arts Press, 1958.

Horner, Robyn. *Rethinking God as Gift: Marion, Derrida and the Limits of Phenomenology*. Perspectives in Continental Philosophy. New York: Fordham University Press, 2001.

Hughes, Cheryl L. "The Primacy of Ethics: Hobbes and Levinas." *Continental Philosophy Review* 31, no. 1 (1998): 79–94.

Irigaray, Luce. *An Ethics of Sexual Difference*. Ithaca: Cornell University Press, 1993.

———. "Questions to Emmanuel Levinas: On the Divinity of Love." Pages 109–18 in *Re-Reading Levinas*, edited by Robert Bernasconi and Simon Critchley. Indianapolis: Indiana University Press, 1991.

Jopling, David. "Levinas on Desire, Dialogue and the Other." *American Catholic Philosophical Quarterly* 65, no. 4 (1991): 405–27.

Kagan, Robert. "Power and Weakness." *Policy Review* 113 (2002): 3–28.

Katz, Claire Elise. "For Love Is as Strong as Death." *Philosophy Today* 45, no. 5 (2001): 124–33.

———. *Levinas, Judaism, and the Feminine: The Silent Footsteps of Rebecca*. Indiana Series in the Philosophy of Religion. Bloomington: Indiana University Press, 2003.

Kearney, Richard. "Desire of God." In Caputo and Scanlon, *God, the Gift, and Postmodernism*, 112–145.

———. "On the Gift." In Caputo and Scanlon, *God, the Gift, and Postmodernism*, 54–78.

Kierkegaard, Sören. *Works of Love: Some Christian Reflections in the Form of Discourses*. New York: Harper, 1962.

Levinas, Emmanuel. *Altérité Et Transcendance*. [Saint-Clément-la-Rivière]: Fata Morgana, 1995.

———. *Alterity and Transcendence*. Translated by Michael B. Smith. European Perspectives. New York: Columbia University Press, 1999.

———. *Autrement Qu'être Ou Au-Delà De L'essence*. Phaenomenologica 54. The Hague: M. Nijhoff, 1974.

———. "Beyond Intentionality in Philosophy." Pages 100–115 in *France Today*, edited by Alan Montefiore. London: Cambridge University Press, 1983.

———. *De Dieu Qui Vient À L'idée*. Paris: J. Vrin, 1982.

———. *Discovering Existence with Husserl*. Edited and translated by Richard A. Cohen and Michael B. Smith. Evanston, Ill.: Northwestern University Press, 1998.

————. "Emmanuel Levinas." Pages 11–24 in *French Philosophers in Conversation*, edited by Raoul Mortley. New York: Routledge, 1991.

————. *Entre Nous: Essais Sur Le Penser-À-L'autre*. Paris: B. Grasset, 1991.

————. *Entre Nous: On Thinking-of-the-Other*. Translated by Michael B. Smith and Barbara Harshav. European Perspectives. New York: Columbia University Press, 1998.

————. *Ethics and Infinity: Conversations with Philippe Nemo*. Edited by Richard A. Cohen. Pittsburgh: Duquesne University Press, 1985.

————. "Ethics and First Philosophy." In Hand, *The Levinas Reader*, 75–87.

————. "Ethics and Politics." In Hand, *The Levinas Reader*, 289–97.

————. *God, Death, and Time*. Translated by Bettina Bergo. Stanford: Stanford University Press, 2000.

————. *Hors Sujet*. [Saint-Clément-la-Rivière]: Fata Morgana, 1997.

————. *In the Time of the Nations*. Translated by Michael B. Smith. London: Athlone Press, 1994.

————. "Is Ontology Fundamental?" Pages 1–10 in *Basic Philosophical Writings*, edited by Adriaan T. Peperzak and Simon Critchley. Bloomington: Indiana University Press, 1996.

————. *Nine Talmudic Readings*. Translated with an introduction by Annette Aronowicz. Bloomington: Indiana University Press, 1990.

————. *Of God Who Comes to Mind*. Translated by Bettina Bergo. Stanford: Stanford University Press, 1998.

————. *On Escape: De L'evasion Emmanuel Levinas*. Stanford: Stanford University Press, 2002.

————. *Otherwise than Being or, Beyond Essence*. Translated by Alphonso Lingis. Martinus Nijhoff Philosophy Texts 3. The Hague/Boston: M. Nijhoff, 1981.

————. *Outside the Subject*. Translated by Michael B. Smith. Stanford: Stanford University Press, 1994.

————. "The Prohibition against Representation and 'the Rights of Man'." Pages 121–30 in *Alterity and Transcendence*.

————. *Proper Names*. Translated by Michael B. Smith. Stanford: Stanford University Press, 1996.

————. *Quatre Lectures Talmudiques [Précédées D'extraits Traduits Du Talmud]*. Collection "Critique". Paris: Éditions de Minuit, 1968.

————. *Totalité Et Infini, Essai Sur L'extériorité*. The Hague: M. Nijhoff, 1961.

————. *Totality and Infinity: An Essay on Exteriority*. Translated by Alphonso Lingis. Duquesne Studies. Pittsburgh: Duquesne University Press, 1969.

Levinas, Emmanuel, and Jacques Rolland. *Dieu, La Mort Et Le Temps, Figures*. Paris: B. Grasset, 1993.

Lifton, Robert Jay. *The Nazi Doctors: Medical Killing and the Psychology of Genocide*. New York: Basic Books, 1986.

Llewelyn, John. *Appositions of Jacques Derrida and Emmanuel Levinas*. Bloomington: Indiana University Press, 2002.

————. "Levinas, Derrida and Others *Vis-a-Vis*." Pages 136–55 in *The Provocation of Levinas Rethinking the Other*. Warwick Studies in Philosophy and Literature. London: Routledge, 1988.

Marion, Jean-Luc. "The Saturated Phenomenon." *Philosophy Today*, vol. 40 (1996): 103–124.

Mauss, Marcel. *The Gift: Forms and Functions of Exchange in Archaic Societies.* Glencoe, Ill.: Free Press, 1954.

Milbank, John. "The Ethics of Self-Sacrifice." *First Things* 91 (1999): 33–38.

Nietzsche, Friedrich Wilhelm. *Thus Spoke Zarathustra: A Book for All and None.* Translated and with a preface by Walter Kaufmann. New York: Viking Press, 1966.

Nygren, Anders. *Agape and Eros.* Chicago: University of Chicago Press, 1982.

O'Connor, Flannery, and Sally Fitzgerald. *The Habit of Being: Letters.* New York: Vintage Books, 1980.

O'Donovan, Oliver. *The Problem of Self-Love in St. Augustine.* New Haven: Yale University Press, 1980.

Olthuis, James H. *Face-to-Face: Ethical Asymmetry or the Symmetry of Mutuality.* Perspectives in Continental Philosophy. New York: Fordham University Press, 1997.

————. *Knowing Other-Wise: Philosophy at the Threshold of Spirituality.* Perspectives in Continental Philosophy. New York: Fordham University Press, 1997.

Outka, Gene H. *Agape: An Ethical Analysis.* Yale Publications in Religion. New Haven: Yale University Press, 1972.

Palmer, Parker J. *To Know as We Are Known.* San Francisco: HarperCollins, 1983.

Peperzak, Adriaan Theodoor. *Beyond: The Philosophy of Emmanuel Levinas.* Northwestern University Studies in Phenomenology and Existential Philosophy. Evanston, Ill.: Northwestern University Press, 1997.

Peperzak, Adriaan T., Simon Critchley, and Robert Bernasconi, eds. *Emmanuel Levinas: Basic Philosophical Writings.* Studies in Continental Thought. Bloomington: Indiana University Press, 1996.

————. *To the Other.* Purdue University Series in the History of Philosophy. West Lafayette, Ind.: Purdue University Press, 1993.

Poirié, François. *Emmanuel Levinas.* Vol. 20, *Qui Êtes-Vous?* Lyon: La Manufacture, 1987.

Ricoeur, Paul. *Oneself as Another.* Translated by Kathleen Blamey. Chicago: University of Chicago Press, 1992.

Robbins, Jill, ed. *Is It Righteous to Be? Interviews with Emmanuel Levinas.* Stanford, Calif.: Stanford University Press, 2001.

Sandford, Stella. *The Metaphysics of Love: Gender and Transcendence in Levinas.* New Brunswick, N.J.: Athlone Press, 2000.

Schrift, Alan D. *The Logic of the Gift: Toward an Ethic of Generosity.* New York: Routledge, 1997.

Silverman, Hugh J. *Philosophy and Desire.* Continental Philosophy. New York: Routledge, 2000.

Simmons, William Paul. "The Third: Levinas's Theoretical Move from an-Archical Ethics to the Realm of Justice and Politics." *Philosophy and Social Criticism* 25, no. 6 (1999): 83–104.

Tocqueville, Alexis de, and Stephen D. Grant. *Democracy in America*. Indianapolis: Hackett, 2000.

Webb, Stephen H. "The Rhetoric of Ethics as Excess: A Christian Theological Response to Emmanuel Levinas." *Modern Theology* 15, no. 1 (1999): 1–16.

Westphal, Merold. "Commanded Love and Divine Transcendence in Levinas and Kierkegaard." In Bloechl, *The Face of the Other and the Trace of God*, 200–223.

———. "Levinas and the Immediacy of the Face." *Faith and Philosophy* 10, no. 4 (1993): 486–99.

———. *Levinas's Teleological Suspension of the Religious*. New York: Routledge, 1995.

———. *Overcoming Onto-Theology*. Bloomington: Indiana University Press, 1999.

———. "The Transparent Shadow: Kierkegaard and Levinas in Dialogue." Pages 265–81 in *Kierkegaard in Post/Modernity*, edited by Martin J. Matustik and Merold Westphal. Bloomington: Indiana University Press, 1995.

———. *Postmodern Philosophy and Christian Thought*. Indiana Series in the Philosophy of Religion. Bloomington: Indiana University Press, 1999.

Wright, Tamra, Peter Hughes, and Alison Ainley. "The Paradox of Morality." Pages 168–80 in *The Provocation of Levinas*. Edited by Robert Bernasconi and David Wood. New York: Routlege, 1988.

Wyschogrod, Edith. *Saints and Postmodernism: Revisioning Moral Philosophy, Religion and Postmodernism*. Chicago: University of Chicago Press, 1990.

Wyschogrod, Edith. *Emmanuel Levinas: The Problem of Ethical Metaphysics*. Perspectives in Continental Philosophy. New York: Fordham University Press, 2000.

Index

159